SECRET
RIO

Manoel de Almeida e Silva, Marcio Roiter and Thomas Jonglez

JonGlez

Manoel de Almeida e Silva

Born in the very traditional neighbourhood of Gamboa, Manoel de Almeida e Silva grew up in Engenho Velho, a long-forgotten name for the area around Tijuca in Rio's Zona Norte. As a journalist and education specialist, he has lived in several countries during twenty-eight years of work with the United Nations, but has now settled in Copacabana. For this guide he has revived personal memories which, combined with his own research and suggestions from friends who are equally enthusiastic about Carioca diversity, aim to help expand the city's tourist itinerary.

Márcio Alves Roiter

Founder of the Instituto Art Déco Brasil (2005), Márcio Alves Roiter is the author of *Rio de Janeiro Art Déco* (Casa da Palavra, 2011), *Art Nouveau e Art Déco: Estilos de Sedução* (Espaço Cultural Península, 2013) and *Um Passeio na História* (with Cynthia Garcia; Arezzo, 2010). Winner of the Cultural Award of the State of Rio de Janeiro, he has organised various exhibitions in Brazil and France, set up the 11th World Congress on Art Deco in Rio in 2011 and acted as a consultant for the restoration of many Art Deco buildings. He was also a speaker at the World Congress on Art Deco in New York (2005), Melbourne (2007) and Montreal (2009).

Bruno Frederick Toussaint Pereira

A researcher specialising in Rio architecture and urban planning, Bruno Frederick Toussaint Pereira has recently contributed to *A Construção do Rio de Janeiro moderno* (Casa da Palavra, 2015), on French architect Joseph Gire, as well as an inventory on Rio de Janeiro monuments published in 2015 by the prefecture.

Pedro da Cunha e Menezes

Diplomat and mountaineer Pedro da Cunha e Menezes has served in Peru, Australia, Kenya, Portugal, South Africa, Albania and Zimbabwe. He has also worked for the Environment Secretariat of Rio prefecture and as director of Tijuca National Park. For two years he was deputy representative of Brazil with the United Nations Environment Programme. He has already covered more than 20,000 km of trails in about 500 national parks of 120 countries.

Carlos Fernando Andrade

An architect and urban planner who trained in 1976 at the Faculty of Architecture and Urbanism of the Federal University of Rio de Janeiro, where he gained an MA (1998) and PhD (2009) in urbanism, Carlos Fernando Andrade has held various administrative functions, such as public works director, Undersecretary of State for Planning, and chair of the State of Rio de Janeiro's National Historic and Artistic Heritage Institute (2011). He also edited the journal *Chão* from 1978 to 1989. In 2009 he received the Pedro Ernesto medal offered by the city council to the Professional of the Year, awarded by the Institute of Architects of Brazil in Rio de Janeiro.

We immensely enjoyed writing the *Secret Rio* guide and hope that, like us, you will continue to discover the unusual, secret and lesser-known facets of this city.

Accompanying the description of some sites, you will find historical information and anecdotes that will let you understand the city in all its complexity. *Secret Rio* also sheds light on the numerous yet overlooked details of places we pass by every day. These details are an invitation to pay more attention to the urban landscape and, more generally, to regard our city with the same curiosity and attention we often feel when travelling…

Comments on this guide and its contents, as well as information on sites not mentioned, are welcome and will help us to enrich future editions.

Don't hesitate to contact us:
- Jonglez Publishing,
  17, boulevard du Roi,
  78000 Versailles, France
- E-mail: info@jonglezpublishing.com

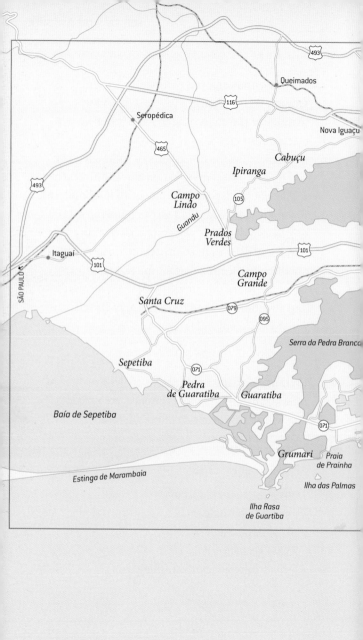

PETRÓPOLIS, BELO HORIZONTE ↑

493

Campos
Elíseos

Santa
Maria

105

São
Bento

Santa
Tereza

p. 268

Ilha de
Paquetá

116

Belford Roxo

040

Ilha do Governador

esquita

Duque
de Caxias

Nilópolis

São João
de Meriti

101 083

Penha

Ilha do
Fundão

Baía de Guanabara

BÚZIOS
↘

Deodoro

angu 079

Madureira

101

Ponte Pres. Costa e Silva

p. 12

Aeroporto Internacional
Rio de Janeiro

Niterói

Aeroporto
Santos Dumont

p. 78

Centro

Meier

RIO DE JANEIRO

Tijuca

079

Foresta de Tijuca

p. 124

Glória

MAC
de Niterói

Botafogo

Pão de Açúcar

Jacarepaguá

p. 206

Copacabana

p. 170

089

Barra da Tijuca

São
Conrado

Ipanema

Joatinga

Ilha Cagarras

Ilha Comprida

Ilha Rasa

Ilha Redonda

p. 236

OCEANO ATLÂNTICO

N

0   5   10 km

CONTENTS

CASTELO, PRAÇA XV

LAPA, CENTRO, GAMBOA, SAÚDE

CONTENTS

BOTAFOGO - FLAMENGO - LARANJEIRAS - CATETE GLORIA - STA TERESA

COPACABANA - URCA

IPANEMA - LEBLON LAGOA - GAVEA
JARDIM BOTANICO HUMAITA

CONTENTS

JOATINGA - SÃO CONRADO - BARRA DA TIJUCA - ZONA OESTE

TIJUCA - SÃO CRISTÓVÃO - ZONA NORTE

Baía de Guanabara

0 200 400 m

N

Pier Mauá

Museu de Amanha

Av. Rodrigues Alves

Cais do Porto

Av. Venezuela

Av. Cabral

SAÚDE

PRAÇA MAJOR VALO

Rua Acre

PRAÇA MAUÁ

Museu de Arte do Rio

Av. Mar. Floriano

Av. Pres. Vargas

Uruguaiana

R. Buenos Aires

LARGO SÃO FR. DE PAULA

Rua Uruguaiana

Av. Rio Branco

R. Dom Gerardo

PRAÇA BARÃO DE LADÁRIO

R. V. de Inhaúma

PRAÇA PIO X

Rua da Alfandega

Rua de Rosário

Rua da Quitanda

Rua da Candelária

Rua Primeiro de Março

Igreja Candelária

4

5

6-7

8

Igreja do Carmo

9

3

Ilha das Cobras

1

PRAÇA D'ARMAS **2**

Rua Arnaldo Luiz

Ilha Fiscal

57

LARGO DO PAÇO

10

PRAÇA QUINZÉ DE NOVEMBRO

Estação das Barcas

11

CENTRO

12

13

14

15

Rua Sete de Setembro

Rua da Assembléia

Rua da Carioca

LARGO DA CARIOCA

Carioca

Av. Nilo Peçanha

PRAÇA M. JONES

Rua San José

PRAÇA MERCADO MUNICIPAL

PRAÇA RUI BARBOSA

Av. República do Chile

Av. República do Paraguai

17

Rua Senador Dantas

R. E. da Veiga

Av. Alm. Barroso

Av. Rio Branco

Rua México

16

R. Araújo Porto Alegre

R. Evaristo da Veiga

19

20-21

PRAÇA FLORIANO

Cinelândia

22

Rua Santa Luzia

Av. Presidente Wilson

25-26

24

23

Av. Pres. Antonio Carlos

PRAÇA DO EXPEDICIONÁRIO

27

Rua Santa Luzia

Av. Mar. Camara

PRAÇA VINTE E DOIS DE ABRIL

Av. Fr. Roosevelt

PRAÇA ITÁLIA

Museu Histórico Nacional

32

29-31

PRAÇA ANTENOR FAGUNDES

Av. General Justo

LAPA

LARGO DA LAPA

Parque Passeio Público

PRAÇA MONROE

18

Av. Beira Mar

PRAÇA DEODORO

Rua Teixeira de Freitas

Av. Angelico Severo

PRAÇA PARIS

PRAÇA PISTÓIA

Museu de Arte Moderna

Av. Infante Dom Henrique

Enseada da Glória

PRAÇA SENADOR CLOVIS SALGADO FILHO

Rua Jardel Jercoli

Aeroporto Santos Dumont

✈

33

Av. Alm. Silvio de Noronha

GLÓRIA

Glória

PRAÇA LUIZ DE CAMÕES

Av. Beira Mar

Av. Infante Dom Henrique

L. DA GLÓRIA

N. S. Glória

Rua da Lapa

Escola Naval

Ilha de Villegaignon

Baía de Guanabara

CASTELO
PRAÇA XV

TIRADENTES' HISTORIC CELL

Hospital Central da Marinha, Ilha das Cobras
Centro
• Open on request Monday to Friday 9am–1pm
• Access: at the far end of Rua Primeiro de Março (left of Rio 450 tunnel),
walk through the military zone as far as Arnaldo Luz bridge and take
the elevator at the Hospital Central da Marinha (Military Hospital), the
entrance to which is opposite the elevator exit

> **One
> of Brazil's most
> significant but
> least-known
> historical sites**

Tiradentes' cell is probably one of Rio's greatest secrets. And yet there's absolutely no indication that it still exists inside the Military Hospital on Ilha das Cobras (Isle of the Snakes) in Guanabara bay.

Yet any morning, from Monday to Friday, you can simply turn up at the hospital entrance and ask to see the cell. Tiradentes was held prisoner there before being transferred to the city's civilian prison (Cadeia Velha), near the current home of the Legislative Assembly of Rio de Janeiro. It was from this prison, demolished in 1922, that the 45-year-old Tiradentes was led to his execution on 21 April 1792 at the junction of Rua Senhor dos Passos and Avenida Passos, not far from what is now Praça Tiradentes (then Campo da Lampadosa). He was hanged, drawn and quartered, and his head displayed on a pillar in the central plaza of Vila Rica (Ouro Preto). His remains were then scattered at Cebolas, Varginha do Lourenço, Barbacena and Queluz, the towns where he'd called for rebellion against the Portuguese colonial power.

Considered a leading member of the revolutionary movement Inconfidência Mineira (see p. 87), Tiradentes was captured on 10 May 1789 in Rua dos Latoeiros (now Rua Gonçalves Dias) while he was expounding his revolutionary ideas on the independence of Brazil.

The cell of three other Inconfidência Mineira members can also be seen at the Morro da Conceição fortress (see p. 87).

MUSEU DO CORPO DE FUZILEIROS NAVAIS

Ilha das Cobras
Centro
• Open Tuesday to Friday 9.30am–4.30pm approximately, also last weekend of the month 1pm–3pm (in which case the military bus departs from the Naval Museum near Praca XV)
• Confirmation by phone recommended: (21) 2126-5053
• Guided tours
• Access: at the far end of Rua Primeiro de Março (left of Rio 450 tunnel), walk through the military zone as far as Arnaldo Luz bridge and take the elevator at the Hospital Central da Marinha. Follow the only road on the right that leads down and turns left. Skirting the military prison, the entrance is on the left
• No flip-flops, and bring a passport or identity card

> **Yes, you can visit the Isle of the Snakes!**

Despite what you might think, you can officially visit Ilha das Cobras (Isle of the Snakes), home of the Brazilian Navy.

You don't need to ask permission, just cross the bridge to the island and climb the steps (or take the impressive elevator) to the highest point – rewarded by unparalleled views of the city and the island itself.

A three-minute walk along the only road will bring you to the Marine Corps Museum, the official excuse to visit the island.

The museum at the historic site of the fort of São José da Ilha das Cobras is a chance to visit what has been the naval headquarters since the Cayenne campaign in French Guiana ended in 1809. On his arrival in Brazil, King Joao VI was minded to punish the French for invading Portugal by taking over French Guiana, which was the scene of heavy fighting before the Brazilian victory of January 1809. The Brigada Real da Marinha (Royal Naval Brigade, renamed the Marine Corps) reached Brazil with the royal court of Portugal in 1808.

Apart from various objects associated with the marines, the museum's main attraction is a tour of several underground passages (one almost 200 m long) dating from the colonial era. They were built by the Portuguese to get around safely on an island that occupied a strategic position, controlling Guanabara bay.

Note also the memorial to marines lost in combat: the roof illustrates the sky of 7 March 1808, the date of Joao VI's arrival in Rio. Each of the 162 stars represents 10 of the 1,622 marines killed.

CENTRO CULTURAL DO MOVIMENTO ESCOTEIRO

❸

Rua Primeiro de Março, Centro
• Tel: (21) 2233-9338 • Open Monday to Friday 10am–5pm
• Metro: Uruguaiana

Brazilian Scouting museum

Quite forgotten on Rua Primeiro de Março, not far from the Candelaria, the Cultural Center of the Scout Movement is a small museum devoted to the history of Brazilian Scouting. Over the two floors of exhibits, you'll learn that Scouting started in Brazil in 1910 thanks to Amélio Azevedo Marques, and see some interesting old posters and various other items relating to the Scout movement founded by Robert Baden-Powell in 1907.

The origin of the movement goes back to the defence of Mafeking, the British military outpost in South Africa during the Second Boer War (1899–1902): army officer Baden-Powell managed to save the town after a seven-month siege by a much larger enemy force. During that time, Baden-Powell had trained the Mafeking youth as messengers, observers, sentries and scouts.

PAINTINGS IN THE NAVE OF IGREJA DE NOSSA SENHORA DA CANDELÁRIA

❹

Praça Pio X
Centro
• Metro: Uruguaiana (Presidente Vargas exit)
• Open: Mon-Fri 7:30am–3:50pm, Saturday 9am–12 noon, Sunday 9am–1pm
• Tel: (21) 2233-2324

> *The church that owes its existence to a storm*

Although consecrated in 1811, the Church of Our Lady of Candelária was not completed until the late 19th century. Dating from the last two decades of that century, the six beautiful paintings on the ceiling of its central nave are often overlooked by visitors. The paintings depict the forgotten story of the founding of the church in the 17th century. A Spanish couple (Antonio Martins Palma and Léonor Gonçalves) were sailing from Europe to Rio on board the *Candelária* when the ship was struck by a dreadful storm. Fearing for their lives, they swore to Our Lady of Candelária that they would build a chapel in her honour if they survived. Once safely in Rio they kept their vow and had a chapel built where Candelária church now stands.

The six panels covering the ceiling from entrance to dome show the voyage of the founders, the violent storm and the blessing of the original chapel. Unlike other paintings in the church, these are not inspired by Bible stories. The panels were designed by Brazilian painter João Zeferino da Costa (1849–1916) who taught at the Academia Imperial de Belas Artes (Imperial Academy of Fine Arts, see p. 214) and are considered to be his masterpiece.

Taking Avenida Presidente Vargas as their point of reference, some people believe the church was built with its back to the city. But in the colonial era it was routine for buildings to face Guanabara Bay, the city's main arrival point. With recent work to revitalise the port of Rio de Janeiro, this geographical relationship with the bay has been brought up to date with the demolition of the raised roadway that used to lead from the church to the shore.

BAS-RELIEF OF THE ASSOCIAÇÃO COMERCIAL ❺ DO RIO DE JANEIRO (ACRJ)

Casa do Empresário
9 Rua Candelária
• www.acrj.org.br • Tel: (21) 2514-1229
• Open Monday to Friday 9am–5pm • Admission free
• Bus: 457, 456, 455, 306, 254

> ## The riches of Brazil carved in stone

Strolling through the historic centre of Rio, it's easy to miss the beautiful bas-relief in the entrance hall of the Trade Association of Rio de Janeiro (Casa do Empresário – House of the Entrepreneur), at the junction of Candelária and Buenos Aires streets. Visit the building during office hours to admire this bas-relief panel entitled *Riquezas do Brasil* (Riches of Brazil), 12 m wide and 7 m high, sculpted by French artist Albert Freyhoffer. At the centre stands the imposing image of Mercury, the Roman god of commerce, on a base that features the Brazilian flag motto, *Ordem e Progresso* (Order and Progress). The panel evokes production and trade while also highlighting the region's exuberant tropical flora and fauna.

The fifteen-storey building, also known as the Palácio do Comércio, was designed by architects Henri Sajous and Auguste Rendu and opened in May 1940. Its three terraces have panoramic views of Guanabara bay.

Before acquiring its own headquarters in 1940, the ACRJ had six temporary homes. A year after the arrival of the Portuguese royal family in 1809, the prince regent Dom João expressed his willingness to construct a commercial square where "merchants could meet, conduct transactions and handle their business affairs". In 1820, Praça do Comércio was inaugurated in the premises now known as Casa França-Brasil (France-Brazil House), close to its present location. It adopted the name Associação Comercial do Rio de Janeiro in 1867.

Besides reproducing the association's coat of arms in the same hall, Freyhoffer designed another bas-relief (2.98 m wide and 3.47 m high) on the terrace. It shows the god Mercury in the foreground, flanked by two muses. Both the terrace and the mural are closed to visitors. You can, however, enjoy fine panoramic views over Guanabara bay from the 13th-floor restaurant.

THE CHRIST STATUE OF IGREJA SANTA CRUZ DOS MILITARES ❻

Rua Primeiro de Março
Centro
• Open Monday to Friday 9am–3.30pm, Saturday 9am–1.30pm
• Tel: (21) 2509-3878

A miraculous Christ

In the Rococo church of the Military Holy Cross, consecrated in 1811, a sculpture of Christ stands behind the main altar. Although, curiously, no information is supplied for visitors, this Christ is revealed to be miraculous, as Augusto Maurício recounts in *Templos Históricos de Rio de Janeiro*, 1845: "*At some point, Portuguese workman Augusto Frederico Corrêa, seeing an image of the dead Christ on the altar, challenged and insulted him. Warned by his workmates, he replied that he had no fear of God and that 'this thing' was just a lump of wood, with no more significance than that. He would only believe in the existence of Christ if he was killed by him at three o'clock that day. Work went on and nobody thought much about what had just happened. But the instant the clock chimed three, a piercing cry was heard from the church. The workman, seized by horrible convulsions, had collapsed in front of the altar of Nossa Senhora das Dores (Our Lady of Sorrows). He was taken to his home at 48 Rua do Senado, where he lay unconscious for three days. On 1 August,*

however, he was found completely healed, with an image of Our Lady of Sorrows clutched in his arms. The whole city was soon aware of these events and on the 12th of the same month, Bishop Dom Manoel do Monte Rodrigues de Araújo went to the scene of the transgression, there to intone prayers in response to the offence given to the statue of Christ. Augusto Frederico Corrêa, on his knees, begged forgiveness for his contempt, expressing his faith and his regrets."

Today, the pardon of the dead Christ is celebrated every 29 July, in memory of the church's statue of Christ, which is placed next to the main altar on that day.

The brotherhood of Santa Cruz dos Militares is the guardian of a number of relics of the Paraguayan War donated by commander-in-chief the Duke of Caxias. According to the brotherhood, there are many other stories of miracles and ghosts. While the present church was being built, bones from the old cemetery were stored in drawers, which would explain why deceased marshals and generals are sometimes heard wandering around the passages. Other than hearing footsteps and voices, many people have claimed that the church organ was playing by itself. In 1923, a fire broke out for no obvious reason on the main altar and rapidly spread, heralding a great disaster. Miraculously, the fire went out at the feet of the statue of Nossa Senhora da Piedade (Our Lady of Piety).

SYMBOLS OF THE PASSION AT IGREJA SANTA CRUZ DOS MILITARES ❼

Rua Primeiro de Março
Centro
• Open Monday to Friday 9am–3.30pm, Saturday 9am–1.30pm
• Tel: (21) 2509-3878

> **Rare representation of the symbols of Christ's Passion**

It's easy to visit the attractive church of the Holy Cross of the Military without noticing that the choir contains some very rare and lovely bas-reliefs of the instruments of Christ's Passion. The following are depicted on both sides of the choir: the inscription INRI ("Jesus of Nazareth King of the Jews"); the crown of thorns; the sword with which Peter cut off the ear of the high priest's servant Malchus and the lantern that enabled him to recognise Christ in the Garden of Gethsemane; the chalice that collected the blood of Christ (which became the Holy Grail); the tunic for which the Roman soldiers threw dice; the rope used to hoist Christ onto the Cross; the lance of the centurion Longinus that pierced his side (see *Secret Rome* in this series of guides); the jug of vinegar used to moisten his lips; the hammer to drive in the nails and the tongs to pull them out; the ladder for the descent from the Cross; the column where Christ was attached for scourging; the cock that crowed at Peter's betrayal; the long pike with its bile-soaked sponge; the thonged whip; the three nails; and the purse containing the coins of Judas' treachery.

Of the instruments of the Passion most frequently depicted around the world, the only ones missing here are a hand sometimes used to symbolise Pontius Pilate; a skull evoking the place of execution, Golgotha (*gulgota* is Aramaic for "skull"); and a sun recalling that at Christ's death there was a solar eclipse lasting three hours.

VERONICA'S VEIL, AN EXTRAORDINARY AND LITTLE-KNOWN RELIC
On the wall at the entrance to the choir, to complement the instruments of the Passion, you'll find an image of the face of Christ that isn't particularly striking. Yet this depicts Veronica's veil, an extraordinary and little-known Christian relic (see following double-page spread).

Above the entrance door, on the street, the inscription *indulgencia plenaria quotidiana* recalls that since 15 April 1923, following a rare privilege, indulgences granted at St Peter's in Rome are also granted to those who come to pray in Santa Cruz dos Militares.

Repeated on the wooden doors of the church are the main instruments of the Passion: the hammer and tongs, together with the crown of thorns and the three nails.

THE EXTRAORDINARY SAGA OF VERONICA'S VEIL

A great many churches possess a copy of a veil on which is imprinted the miraculous image of the face of Christ. The origin of this image is to be found in the Gospels of Mark (5: 25-34), Matthew (9: 20-22) and Luke (8: 43-48), which all relate the story of a woman who was healed of a haemorrhage by Jesus. Around the year 400, the Bishop of Lydia named her Berenike, a little before the apocryphal Gospel of Nicodemus (circa 450) finally referred to her as Veronica. The name seems to derive from "vero" and "icona", meaning "true image", while the personality of Veronica was embellished, gradually departing from the miraculously healed woman. In the 7th century, another apocryphal text, The Death of Pilate, spoke of Veronica as a confidante of Jesus to whom he had given the veil on which his face was imprinted.

Towards 1160, the canon of Saint Peter's Basilica in Rome, Pietro Mallius, put forward the hypothesis that this legend had arisen when, seeing Christ carrying his Cross to Golgotha, a woman removed her veil to wipe his brow and the image of his face was miraculously imprinted on it. This notion took root and little by little it was established as the true version of this rare and miraculous acheiropoieta (an image not made by the hand of man).

Still according to legend, Veronica's veil was first reported to be kept in Saint Peter's Basilica in 1287, although Pope Celestine III (1191-1198) had previously mentioned the existence of such a shroud. The veil may have been sold during the sack of Rome in 1527, but, as often happens with relics, it soon reappeared and was again noted in the relics hall in the 17th century, although some claimed that the face imprinted on the veil was that of a peasant named Manopello.

The cathedral of Jaen, in Spain, also claims to possess the authentic veil of Veronica.

comandada por *Custódio José de Melo*, o
dramaticamente lançada para fora de seu
atingida por uma bala disparada por um dos
os navios da esquadra revoltada contra o
balaço, profanador, a Estátua foi arrojada
u pelo telhado e foi cair no solo. A alma
grande abalo, mas ressurgiu fortalecida em
mentado de boca em boca durante muito
sofrido. Apenas o polegar e o indicador da
arrega no regaço, como uma tocha luminosa
sim, ficava ela praticamente ilesa. A bala, já
na parede e onde ainda hoje se acha, e a

QUE EM
18 93
ATTINGIU
...

SHELL IN THE IGREJA DE NOSSA SENHORA DA LAPA DOS MERCADORES ❽

Sacristy, Igreja de Nossa Senhora da Lapa dos Mercadores
35 Rua do Ouvidor
• Open Monday to Friday 8am to 2pm
• Metro: Uruguaiana
• Tel: (21) 2509-2339

Statue hit by a shell

There's an unexpected sight in the sacristy of the Traders' Church of Our Lady of Lapa – a shell embedded in the wall.

During the 1893 armed forces mutinies against the Brazilian government, a shell fired by the battleship *Aquidabã* hit the church tower and felled the statue that now stands in the sacristy, next to the shell. Despite falling over 25 m, the statue wasn't greatly damaged: only a few fingers of the left hand were broken off plus a piece of the base, which was recovered and repaired.

Many people regarded this as a miracle, and some still attend church today to pray and petition "Our Lady of the Grotto" on the strength of this incident.

The cult of Nossa Senhora da Lapa is attributed to another alleged miracle that took place in Portugal during the Muslim occupation of the Iberian peninsula. The story goes that the nuns of a convent in the parish of Quintela were afraid of the Moors and fled, hiding an image of Our Lady in a small cave among the rocks. Years later, a young mute girl recovered her speech when she stumbled on the hidden statue. A chapel was built at the site and the cult of Nossa Senhora da Lapa was born.

Back in Rio, a group of merchants who worshipped the same saint at an oratory in Rua dos Mercadores decided to have a church built in 1747. The work took until 1771 and it wasn't until 1812, when the original oratory was demolished, that the statue of Nossa Senhora da Lapa was transferred to the new church. This church, in its current form, is the result of the great reform of 1870 that transformed it into an exemplary harmonious blend of the Baroque and neoclassical. Around this time a tower was added, together with the sculpture that was damaged shortly afterwards. The tower was rebuilt in 1895 and the city's first belfry installed there.

Rua do Ouvidor already existed in 1578 as Desvio do Mar, since when it has had some twenty names. The most recent dates from 1745, when an *ouvidor* (mediator) was working in the locality with the task of listening (*ouvir* in Portuguese) to people's complaints and bringing them before the king.

STATUE OF ST EMERENTIANA   **9**

Igreja de Nossa Senhora do Carmo
Rua Primeiro de Março
• Open Monday to Friday 8am–4pm, Saturday 8am–11am
• Tel: (21) 2242-4828
• www.igrejanscarmorj.com.br

> *A rare image of the great-grandmother of Jesus*

To the right of the choir of the magnificent church of Our Lady of Mount Carmel, an unobtrusive statue is easily missed. The work of an anonymous 18th-century artist, it is a rare representation of St Emerentiana, the great-grandmother of Jesus, according to apocryphal texts. Be careful not to confuse her with another St Emerentiana (or St Emerentia), martyred in the 4th century AD.

With her right arm Emerentiana is holding St Anne, and her left arm supports her daughter, mother of the Virgin Mary. Mary herself holds Jesus in her arms.

St Anne is shown slightly larger than Mary, perhaps indicating her seniority over her daughter. The rich clothes of the different characters indicate their noble and sacred origin.

A stained-glass window at Sainte-Anne-d'Auray church in Brittany (France) also features St Emerentiana.

HOW DO WE KNOW ABOUT ST EMERENTIANA?

Most of the information on St Emerentiana, who is not mentioned in the Bible, comes from several sources. First are the mystical visions of St Colette of Corbie (1381–1447?), Anne-Catherine Emmerick (1774–1824) and Maria Valtorta (1897–1961). Other sources are Paul Victor Charland's *Le Culte de Saint Anne en Occident* (The Cult of Saint Anne in the West), published in 1920, and *La vie et les gloires de sainte Anne, tirées d'auteurs anciens et modernes* (The Life and Glories of Saint Anne, from Ancient and Modern Authors).

Note that Anne and Joachim (parents of the Virgin Mary) are not mentioned in the canonical Gospels: they only appear for the first time in the *Protevangelium of James*, an apocryphal "pre-Gospel" of the 2nd century AD. St Cyril of Alexandria, in the 5th century, picked up this information before *The Golden Legend* (a 13th-century collection of hagiographies by Jacobus de Voragine) spoke of a sister of Anne's, thought to have been called Hismarian, the mother of Elizabeth and thus the grandmother of St John the Baptist.

According to these sources, Emerentiana was born in the village of Sepphoris (Saphora), north of Mount Carmel, where she used to go and meet the disciples of the prophets Elijah and Elysium. It was also on Mount Carmel that Elijah built a chapel dedicated to the Virgin who was supposed to bear a child. Among these disciples was a certain Archos, with whom she regularly kept the mysteries of the faith, who prophesied that she would marry and give birth to the woman who was to be the mother of Christ.

At the age of 18, Emerentiana married Stolan, a man of royal blood, who gave her a daughter whom she named Hismarian. When this daughter reached the age of 15, she married Eliud. They had a daughter named Elizabeth, who became the wife of the high priest Zacharias and mother of John the Baptist. Hismarian also gave birth to a child named Emin, who counted among his descendants St Servatius, the first bishop of Tongeren.

The years passed and it was only at an advanced age that Emerentiana and Stolan saw themselves fulfil the prophecy of Archos. One day, in a mystical vision, they saw at the head of their bed four golden letters forming the name of Anne, who was born not long afterwards.

GENERAL OSÓRIO'S RIDING GEAR

Praça XV
Centro
• Metro: Carioca

> ## Why the bootless statue?

You'll need to be especially perceptive to spot that the great equestrian statue of General Osório (see below), in the centre of Praça XV, shows the general wearing ordinary dress shoes rather than his customary boots. But there's an explanation for this apparent "error".

After researching this commission, sculptor Rodolfo Bernardelli chose suitable clothes and accessories: uniform and riding boots. After completing the model, which is kept at the Historical Museum (not on public display), Bernardelli showed it to Osório's daughter, who explained that her father hadn't worn boots since 1866. During the battle of Passo da Pátria, after 24 hours of torrential rain, the general's legs had swelled so much he couldn't get his waterlogged boots off. He ordered them to be cut off so he could get back to the fray. He won the battle, but subsequently suffered from a leg inflammation that meant he couldn't wear boots for the rest of his life. After listening to the daughter's tale, Bernardelli decided to stick to historical reality and depicted the general in dress shoes rather than riding boots.

The monument was unveiled under the Republic as a tribute to a general of the Empire. It was well received because Osório was greatly appreciated. Public contributions helped to fund this work and some 40,000 people took part in the inauguration ceremony on 12 November 1894.

The battle of Passo da Pátria and the famous battle of Tuiuti – Osório's great military feats in the Paraguayan War – are shown in two bas-reliefs on the base of the statue. The one pictured (8 m high and weighing 5,700 kg) was cast in Paris by Ateliers Thibaut in 1892, from the bronze of cannons captured from the Paraguayans.

Manuel Luís Osório – general, member of parliament, senator, baron, count and Marquis of Erval – was born in the Brazilian state of Rio Grande do Sul in 1808. A hero of the Paraguayan War (1864–1870), he died in Rio in 1879, at his home at what is now number 303 Rua de Riachuelo. His last residence was converted into a museum in 1983 and is now the home of the Academia Brasileira de Filosofia (Brazilian Academy of Philosophy). The house, listed as national heritage, is clad with Portuguese *azulejos*.

SECRETS OF IGREJA DE SÃO JOSÉ

⑪

Avenida Presidente Antônio Carlos
Centro
• Open Monday to Friday 8am–12 noon and 2pm–5pm, Sunday 8.30am–11am
• Tel: (21) 2533-4545

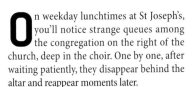

A saintly surprise

On weekday lunchtimes at St Joseph's, you'll notice strange queues among the congregation on the right of the church, deep in the choir. One by one, after waiting patiently, they disappear behind the altar and reappear moments later.

Visitors have to stand in line like everyone else and venture behind the altar to admire or pray before a spectacular sculpture of the last moments of the life of Joseph, with Mary standing at the bedside of a recumbent Joseph, who looks grizzled and defeated, and Jesus at his other side raising a hand in blessing.

The faith demonstrated by believers, as well as the quality and realism of the carving, make this a brief encounter (don't linger in front of the statues, given the number of people waiting) one of intimacy and intense reverence.

Although the 1842 interior is a typical late Rococo work, the original church was built on this same site in the 16th century by the hermit Egas Muniz. In 1659, the city's most sacred relics were moved so that the congregation didn't have to face the gruelling climb to attend the original cathedral on Morro do Castelo (Castle hill). St Joseph's took in the baptismal font, the tabernacle and the patron saint of the city.

The sound of the church bells is famous, thanks to an 1883 carillon that plays a range of tunes.

"AO REI DOS MÁGICOS" BUILDING

116 Rua do Ouvidor
• Metro: Carioca

A neo-Egyptian building where Brazil's first phone was made

There was a time when the streets of Rio were graced with eclectic buildings of various "neo-styles" to give it a cosmopolitan image: Romanesque, Gothic Revival, neo-Baroque, neo-Rococo, neo-Persian, neo-Moresque and neo-Egyptian.

At the junction of Avenida Rio Branco and Rua do Ouvidor is a particularly striking neo-Egyptian building with two statues of Egyptian servants holding up amphorae of incense on its second-floor balcony. The railings are decorated with winged scarabs and the fourth floor has arched balconies that rear upwards and outwards.

This building, dating from the 19th century before the opening of Avenida Rio Branco by Pereira Passos (1903–1905), was home to the store known as Ao Rei dos Mágicos (At the King of Magicians), where in 1877 Brazil's first phone was made. Rio was the first city outside the United States to have this technology.

Emperor Pedro II had previously visited the 1876 Philadelphia World's Fair that celebrated the centenary of US independence. On 25 June, he turned his attention to a Scottish inventor who wasn't attracting much interest: Alexander Graham Bell, who invited him to inspect his device. Bell began to recite Shakespeare at which, according to some historians, the emperor exclaimed: "My God, it speaks!"

Such royal enthusiasm encouraged the rapid expansion of this scientific breakthrough around the country. The following year, the Ao Rei dos Mágicos branch of the Rodle & Chaves society was granted the concession to install telephone lines in the city of Rio de Janeiro.

A publication of the same year, 1877, reveals that the firm also supplied "Indian flares", "megaphones", "lightning rods", "telegraphs" and "preparations to kill rats, cockroaches and all insects", besides conjuring tricks and "electric collars for children". In later logbooks, the "Casa Scientífica e Original" even announced its "telephones". In May 1878 the weekly *O Telephone* was launched.

The scarab is associated with Khepri, the divine manifestation of the early morning sun, and thus symbol of the rebirth of the soul. The Egyptians frequently used it as a talisman.

There is another neo-Egyptian building at 40/42 Rua Pedro Alves, Santo Cristo (see p. 81).

BAS-RELIEF BY ORESTES ACQUARONE

Edifício Guinle
135 Avenida Rio Branco, corner of Rua Sete de Setembro, Centro
• Metro: Carioca

Modernity in motion

In the hubbub of Avenida Rio Branco, the Guinle building (1928) is one of the few major Art Deco buildings in Rio. In addition to its steel guardrails with their zigzag lines, the gallery entrance hall has an ode to "modernity in motion". The golden stucco painting by Orestes Acquarone (see box), above the reception desk, celebrates speed in its depiction of various means of transport: car, ship, locomotive ...

Although ships and locomotives were not of course new inventions, in the 20th century they began to achieve speeds that no one had previously thought possible. In 1900 a car could travel at 20 km/h: by 1930 it could reach 100 km/h. In 1900, aviation was still a dangerous experiment ... Santos Dumont knew that well.

And so in 1928, Europe and Brazil were already connected thanks to the French airmail service, and in 1922 Sacadura Cabral and Gago Coutinho (both Portuguese) had made the first aerial crossing of the Atlantic from Lisbon to Rio de Janeiro. Streets in Rio's Gamboa and Laranjeiras neighbourhoods are named after them.

FIRST SKYSCRAPER ON AVENIDA RIO BRANCO

The Guinle building, a Gusmão, Dourado & Baldassini project, was the first skyscraper on Avenida Rio Branco. It marks the beginning of the second generation of buildings on the former Avenida Central, the property of Eduardo Guinle. He was born after the demolition of the building by Junnuzzi & Irmão in the early 1930s, inaugurating Avenida Central.

ORESTES ACQUARONE

Orestes Acquarone, Uruguayan designer, graphic artist and sculptor (Montevideo, 1875–1952), spent a long time in Buenos Aires before settling in Rio in 1922, where he worked with some of the city's best-known publications: *Ilustração brasileira*, *O Malho* and *La Semana*. In 1926, he took up sculpture and exhibited several times at Rio's national exhibition of fine art.

GONÇALVES DIAS MEDALLION

⑭

40 Rua Gonçalves Dias
• Metro: Carioca

> *Medallion commemorating the writer of the famous "Song of Exile" poem*

A few steps from the celebrated Confeitaria Colombo café, on the right above the entrance to the Galeria dos Empregados do Comércio, is a medallion bearing the profile and name of Gonçalves Dias. The street is called after him as he lived in the house that used to stand here.

Antônio Gonçalves Dias was born in 1823 in the state of Maranhão, the son of a Portuguese merchant and a mixed-descent mother from northern Brazil. He studied law in Portugal, where he rubbed shoulders with the great names of Portuguese literature at that time: Almeida Garrett, Alexandre Herculano and Feliciano de Castilho. At the age of 20, feeling homesick, he wrote *Canção do Exilio* (Song of Exile) – perhaps the best-known poem in Brazilian literature.

The palm branch and dove on the medallion evoke these lines:

My land has palm trees where the *sabiá* [native dove] sings;

The birds that sing here do not sing as they do there ...

Our skies have more stars, our valleys have more flowers,

Our forests have more life. Our lives have more love.

On his return to Brazil, Gonçalves Dias carved out a brilliant career in his home town and later in Rio de Janeiro, then the capital city. He taught Latin and history, wrote for various literary journals and was patron of the 15th chair at the Brazilian Academy of Letters (see p. 53). He also held government posts, and on his way home from an official trip to Europe in 1864 he drowned when the *Ville de Boulogne* was shipwrecked off the coast of Maranhão.

Lines from his "Song of Exile" are included in the Brazilian national anthem.

AREZZO'S STAINED-GLASS WINDOW

13 Rua Gonçalves Dias
• Metro: Carioca
• www.arezzo.com.br

An Art Deco masterpiece

Almost opposite the famous Confeitaria Colombo, the Arezzo store has been installed since 2012 in a beautiful mid-19th century house at number 13 Rua Gonçalves Dias – the street that Brazilian author Machado de Assis called "the painful road of poor husbands" (the best shopping in the city since colonial times).

The building was home to an ice-cream parlour in the late 19th century, then to Loja das Sedas (silk merchants) in the 1930s (when the fabrics were shown by models parading on a double staircase wearing the latest creations) and, between 1930 and 2010, the famous Casa Daniel (House of Daniel). Specialising in gifts, this was for many years one of the best shops of its kind in Rio. In the early 20th century, it was very simple for future brides planning the great event: wish list at Casa Daniel, dress from Casa Canada and buffet reception at Confeitaria Colombo, all very close to each other.

When businessman Anderson Birman decided to renovate the building, which had been in a very poor state of repair for several years, he found that all Loja das Sedas' interior decor was still intact: a beautiful "Hollywood" staircase, elegant wooden furniture, but above all an Art Deco stained-glass window of exceptional quality at the head of the stairs. This large window depicting silkworms is attributed to the country's leading Art Deco graphic designer, José Carlos de Brito e Cunha, known as J. Carlos.

During the renovations, which took two years, relics from the building's previous occupants were found, such as the 19th-century Villeroy-Boch *azulejos* that can still be seen today on the ground floor – the pleasing result of some urban archaeology.

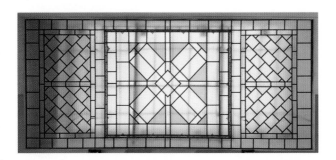

SANTA BARBARA E AS OPERARIAS CERAMIC PANEL 🔟

Museu National das Belas Artes (MNBA)
199 Avenida Rio Branco, Centro
• Open Tuesday to Friday 10am–6pm, Saturdays, Sundays and public holidays, 12 noon–5pm • Admission: R$8, concessions R$4, free Sundays • Tel: (21) 2219-8474
• www.mnba.gov.br/6_programacao/programacao.htm
• Metro: Cinelândia

From tunnel to museum

The monumental ceramic tile panel depicting St Barbara and the Workers stands in a courtyard of the National Museum of Fine Arts that is closed to the public. It can, however, be viewed from two galleries of reproductions on the first floor. This 1963 artwork by renowned Brazilian painter and engraver Djanira is a tribute to the eighteen workers killed during the construction of the Catumbi-Laranjeiras tunnel (also known as the Santa Barbara tunnel) between 1947 and 1963.

The panel was originally commissioned to decorate a chapel (now gone), built in a sort of open grotto above the tunnel roof after a rock fall during the construction work.

As access to this chapel dedicated to St Barbara, the patron saint of miners, was particularly difficult (cars can't stop in the tunnel and pedestrians are banned), the panel was hidden for almost twenty years, suffering from the effects of damp, heat and pollution.

In 1985 it was taken away for renovation, but was stored in a crate for several years before being restored and installed at the MNBA in 1996.

Amid abstract designs, this ceramic panel – one of the masterpieces of Brazilian mural art – shows the saint wrapped in a cloak, surrounded by angels and workers with their tools. Over 5,000 glazed *azulejos*, in shades ranging from dark blue to white, cover an area of more than 130 m^2.

At the opening of the Santa Barbara tunnel chapel, a stele was installed with an inscription in honour of the dead workers: "You who pass along this way, which our deaths have opened up through the rock, ask St Barbara that we should know life by the side of God."

DJANIRA, THE ARTIST WHO DIDN'T WANT TO BE KNOWN AS SUCH

Born to a modest family deep in the state of São Paulo, Djanira da Motta e Silva (1914–1979) moved to Rio in the late 1930s. There she opened a lodging house in Santa Teresa that was frequented by many artists. She then began to draw regularly. An "artist" despite herself (she refused this label), she explained one day during an interview: "I didn't want to be called an 'artist'. I thought that to be an artist, I'd have to know many things that I didn't know." The MNBA holds 814 of her works (the largest extant collection).

LICEU LITERÁRIO PORTUGUÊS *AZULEJOS*

118 Rua Senador Dantas, Centro
• Open office hours
• Metro: Carioca

Although the neo-Manueline building of the Portuguese Literary Lyceum, just opposite the Largo da Carioca, is well known to Cariocas, the lovely tiled panels in the lobby are much less so. Yet it's well worth a visit to enjoy these scenes from Portugal's history, including the victory of the first king of Portugal, Afonso Henriques, at the battle of Ourique in 1139.

The Literary Lyceum is a non-profit association founded in 1868 by a group of Portuguese in order to spread their culture and promote education and training. This laudable initiative is still active today. It would be good if modern Brazil were as attentive to the education of its population as the founders of the association were … The present building opened in 1938.

MEDALLION OF EDIFÍCIO BRASILIA

311 Avenida Rio Branco
Centro
• Metro: Cinelândia

A bove the main door of the Brasilia building – a 1940s project by French architects Viret & Marmorat – a pretty medallion depicts an indigenous woman

A little Art Deco gem

with a bow, Sugarloaf Mountain in the background. The medallion is signed Humberto Cozzo (1900–1981), a leading Brazilian Art Deco sculptor from São Paulo. It is a hymn to Brazil, its nature and its peoples, which so fascinated Europeans in the early 20th century.

Working throughout the country, Cozzo was the official sculptor of the Vargas government. He also designed the bas-reliefs on the façade and in the lobby of the Ministry of Finance.

The main door of the Brasilia building is the work of Raymond Subes, master of French artistic ironwork.

MUSEU JUDAICO DO RIO DE JANEIRO

90 Rua Mexico, 1st floor
• Admission: R$10
• Open Monday to Thursday 10am—4pm, Friday 10am—2pm
• Metro: Cinelândia
• Tel: (21) 2524-6451
• www.museujudaico.org.br

> ## Osvaldo Aranha: a Brazilian behind the creation of Israel

The small and welcoming Jewish Museum, founded in 1977, aims to preserve the memory of Jewish immigration to Rio. So a visit is an opportunity to research the subject as well as to update your knowledge of Judaism, as the objects on display are often accompanied by explanatory sheets on the cultural and historical context of Jewish rituals and traditions.

You'll learn about the important role played by the Brazilian Osvaldo Aranha (1894–1960) in the creation of the State of Israel: as President of the UN General Assembly, he signed the mandate on the partition of Palestine (or what was left of it, Transjordan having already been established in 1922 in part of ancient Palestine) at the 29 November 1947 session. The mandate was directly linked to the creation of Israel in 1948, which earned Aranha the eternal gratitude of Jews around the world, although his role in the government of Getúlio Vargas was ambiguous: it was he who, in 1943, circulated a note around the Brazilian embassies of various European countries on the need to severely restrict the number of entry visas issued to Jews. Aranha, Minister of External Relations at the time, even rather abruptly dismissed the Brazilian consul in Marseille, Luiz Martins de Souza Dantas, who had authorised visas for Jews.

The museum also has a collection of menorah and chanukiah that demonstrates the difference between the two.

The menorah is a candelabrum with seven branches, as originally made by Moses: it symbolises the burning bush he witnessed on Mount Sinai. It became one of the artefacts of the Tabernacle, then of the Temple of Jerusalem, and is one of the symbols of Judaism.

The chanukiah is a candelabrum with nine branches (eight plus one) used by Jews during the celebration of Hanukkah, the festival of light: this commemorates the liberation of the Temple of Jerusalem following the Maccabean revolt against the Seleucids. According to tradition, the victorious Judeans found only a small flask of pure olive oil to kindle the Temple menorah. This oil, which would normally have burned for only one day, miraculously lasted for eight days.

PORTINARI PANELS AT PALÁCIO GUSTAVO CAPANEMA ㉔

16 Rua da Imprensa, Castelo
- Tel: (21) 2220-1490
- Open Monday to Friday 10am–6pm • Admission free
- Metro: Cinelândia

Little-known Carioca masterpieces

Although Capanema Palace is an icon of modern architecture, the second floor is home to unknown works on Carioca themes (all commissioned for the building) by modernist painter Cândido Portinari (1903–1962).

At the elevator exit is the *Jogos infantis* (Children's Games) exhibition, a tribute to the huge mural of the same name that dominates the space and shows typical childhood activities from the Brazilian interior.

Admire the tubular steel sofas, probably by Lúcio Costa, and Oscar Niemeyer's vast carpet. And have a look through the windows to discover the external architecture – a powerful example of Brazilian modernism.

Just next door is the Portinari room, with a series of the artist's paintings that form a large mural depicting the cycles of the country's economy:

pau-brasil, sugar cane, cattle, ore prospecting, cotton, tea, coffee, cocoa, iron, palm and rubber.

In the Gilberto Freyre conference room on the lower floor, two panels evoke the early days of education under the Jesuits. This set of frescoed panels is typical of Portinari's work, highlighting his awareness of social issues.

On the second floor, paintings from the abstract series *Os quatro elementos* (The Four Elements) can be seen. As these are offices, access is limited, but with a little luck you can catch a glimpse of them ... *Ar* (Air) is in the former office of Minister Gustavo Capanema (1900–1985), while *Água* (Water) is in the office of his principal private secretary, poet Carlos Drummond de Andrade (1902–1987). The other two elements, *Fogo* (Fire) and *Terra* (Earth), are in adjacent rooms.

At street level, Portinari's *azulejos* decorate the exterior of the building – they all feature marine motifs. Specialist Carlos Zílio claims this work is not only "the most important by the artist, but also one of the most expressive of modernism". There's a story attached to their creation. When Capanema discovered the marine panels decorated with fish, he considered the result "aesthetically unsatisfactory". This remark is said to have been elicited by the prominent facial features of both minister and fish. Portinari made some replacement tiles, which would explain the starfish that appear on one of the panels.

CAPANEMA HANGING GARDENS

㉑

Palácio Gustavo Capanema
16 Rua da Imprensa, Castelo
• Open Monday to Friday 10am–6pm
• Tel: (21) 2220-1490 • Admission free
• Metro: Cinelândia

> *A roof garden hidden from view*

On the second floor of Capanema Palace, a roof garden (which can't be seen from the street) is one of the principles of modernism set out by Swiss architect Le Corbusier (1887–1965). This underrated garden with its sinuous lines, designed by landscape architect Roberto Burle Marx (1909–1994), only features Brazilian plant species. Among them stands the red granite *Mulher sentada* (Seated Woman) statue, the work of Adriana Janacópulos (1897–1978). The garden is similar to another at street level, also by Burle Marx, with lines mimicking waves interacting with Portinari's marine-inspired *azulejo* panels (see p. 48). There's also a roof garden on the 16th floor, with limited access, which in addition to offering a fine view lets you appreciate the "conversation" between the hanging garden and its counterpart outside.

A SOPHISTICATED STATUE

Modernist sculptor Celso Antônio (1896–1984) created the *Maternidade* (Maternity) statue that stood at the head of the palace's lovely spiral staircase until 1952, before disappearing and then reappearing some months later. We now know that Lúcio Costa, then working for the Heritage Department, had asked for the statue to be removed because he considered it unsuitable for the site. It was offered to the town hall and installed in a garden at Praia de Botafogo near the Church of the Immaculate Conception, where it still can be seen today.

THE MINISTER WHO WANTED A MODERN BUILDING

The palace, built between 1936 and 1945 as the seat of the Ministry of Education and Health (MES) – now the Ministry of Education and Culture (MEC) – is listed as national heritage. It is known locally as the "MEC building" despite being named after the minister responsible, Gustavo Capanema. The project provoked heated debate. Despite receiving thirty-four tenders, Capanema (who wanted a modern building) caused controversy by ignoring the result and separately commissioning Lúcio Costa, one of the modern architects excluded from the tender. Other architects incorporated into Costa's team included Oscar Niemeyer, Jorge Moreira, Afonso Reidy, Carlos Leão and Ernani Vasconcelos, who followed the modernist principles of Le Corbusier. Other than the roof garden, modernist features include the rows of 10 m high pillars that create an open public space below; the glass façade opposite the protective sun canopy; granite blind gables; the spiral staircase leading to the upper floor; and modern sculptures.

GUIDED TOUR OF ACADEMIA BRASILEIRA DE LETRAS

203 Avenida Presidente Wilson, Castelo
• Metro: Cinelândia
• Guided tour on Mondays, Wednesdays and Fridays, 2pm–3pm, lasts about an hour • Free
• Reservations required: (21) 3974-02526 or visita.guiada@academia.org.br

A great time was had by all

Three times a week, you can visit the charming interiors of the Brazilian Academy of Letters. The tour is led by professional actors who recount the history of the academy and from time to time recite famous passages from Brazilian literature, such as the Gonçalves Dias *Song of Exile* (see p. 39).

The visit may seem a bit kitsch at first (the actors are in late 19th-century costume), but you have a great time: the actors are very good, sometimes funny, as the representatives of the Academy who welcome visitors, and you learn something too. Note that there are Rio school students on almost all the tours, so good humour and a little horseplay are to be expected.

A VESTIGE OF THE EXPOSITION OF 1922

The building is one of the few vestiges of the Independence Centenary International Exposition of 1922 (see following double-page spread). Built in 1922 as the French pavilion, it is a copy of the Petit Trianon at Versailles (see photo). The building was presented to the Brazilian Academy of Letters by France in 1923, along with some of its fittings.
The small garden at the back was designed by Burle Marx.

Also part of the Academy, the Palácio Austregésilo de Athayde (named after an academician), next door, was built in 1979 on the site of the former British pavilion at the 1922 Expo. Reservations are theoretically required but can be made for five minutes later... You can visit the second-floor area devoted to Machado de Assis (one of the greatest Brazilian authors of all time), with memorabilia and furniture from the writer's last home. The first-floor Centro de Memória (Centre of Memories) has a collection of historical photographs relating to the Academy. Open Monday to Friday 9am–6pm.

EXPOSIÇÃO INTERNACIONAL DO CENTENÁRIO DO BRASIL (1922–1923)

The Independence Centenary International Exposition was the first World's Fair to be held after the 1914–1918 war.

More than twenty pavilions were built, as well as two monumental gateways and an amusement park. Initially designed to be a national Expo, like that of 1908 which was also held in Rio (see p. 200), it benefited from the participation of fourteen countries.

More than 6,000 national and international exhibitors were represented. The Brazilian section of the exposition stretched from Praça XV to the former fort at Calabouço (Calaboose Point, now the National Historical Museum).

The pavilions were built along what was then called Avenida das Nações (now Avenida Presidente Wilson). An estimated 3 million visitors attended, 200,000 of them on opening day.

The exposition transformed the urban space and encouraged the use of new techniques and building materials. Ironically, this event celebrating the end of the colonial period also sanctioned neocolonialism as a national style.

The celebrations were marked by the opening speech of President Epitácio Pessoa (1865–1942) – the country's first radio broadcast. A special lighting system had been installed for nocturnal visits and, in another first for a World's Fair, films were screened.

Many of the pavilions were built on recent landfill from the levelling of Morro do Castelo (see p. 61-62) for the Expo site.

Exposição do Centenario - 1922

DIVERSÕES

OTHER REMINDERS OF THE 1922-1923 EXPO

Apart from the Petit Trianon (see p. 53), two more buildings were constructed for the International Exposition to commemorate the centenary of Brazil's independence, held between September 1922 and July 1923. Now the Museu da Imagem et do Som (MIS – Museum of Image and Sound) and the Centro Cultural do Ministério da Saúde (CCMS – Cultural Centre of the Ministry of Health), both in Praça Marechal Âncora, they were used as the Federal District Pavilion and Statistics Pavilion respectively.

A group of three former military buildings renovated to accommodate the Industries Pavilion are now home to the Museu Histórico Nacional (MHN – National Historical Museum). The United States Consulate (147 Avenida Presidente Wilson) stands on the site where the North American Pavilion was built.

The Pavilhão Carlos Lopes, where Portuguese industrial products were exhibited, was relocated to Lisbon in 1932. (See *Secret Lisbon* in this series of guidebooks.)

SANTA LUZIA CAR-PARK WALL

In front of 255 Rua Santa Luzia
• Metro: Cinelândia
• Open 24/7

A historic wall recovered

Anyone who uses the Santa Luzia underground car park will already know about this. But passers-by strolling along the sidewalks will never guess that the remains of a historic wall can be seen down there.

There was a time when the waves almost lapped against the nearby church of Santa Luzia. There was even a beach of that name. Since then, the chunks of land successively reclaimed from the sea have gradually filled the space between church and ocean.

The first embankment was built under the administration of Pereira Passos, in the early 20th century, to make way for Avenida Beira Mar. To contain the boulevard and protect it from the force of the waves, the prefecture built a retaining wall that followed the shoreline from Santa Casa da Misericórdia in the direction of Glória.

With the razing of Morro do Castelo to construct the embankment where the 1922 Independence Centenary International Exposition was staged (see preceding page), this wall has disappeared, and is now buried and forgotten.

However, in the 2000s the prefecture authorised the construction of several underground car parks, one below the under-used lanes of Avenida Presidente Antônio Carlos.

When the workers started digging, they were faced with a huge obstacle. Once the wall had been identified, a thorny issue remained: how to preserve this archaeological find while allowing the parking lot to go ahead? The solution was to open a breach in the wall wide enough for vehicles and to preserve the two side sections, the last witnesses to a contentious maritime project that had left little trace.

In order to pour the concrete needed to surface the car park, two large sections of the wall had to be lifted to the surface and then reinstalled once the floor had been laid, using two massive cranes.

The wall turned out to be so well built that the mortar in the joints didn't even crack, meaning that the sections could be raised and lowered in one piece.

Go down into the parking lot today, via the stairs or the elevator, and you can still see them on the nearest part of the church.

For more about the land Rio has reclaimed from the sea, see the following double-page spread.

RIO: A CITY BUILT ON LAND LARGELY RECLAIMED FROM THE SEA

The Rio landscape has changed enormously since the arrival of the first settlers: to enlarge the city, and sometimes for health reasons, beaches, ponds, swamps and even rivers were filled in. Hills were levelled, and the city created new vistas.

In the early 18th century, Lagoa de Santo Antônio (Saint Anthony's Lagoon), which joined the sea at high tide, was filled in and became what is now Largo da Carioca. The site of Rua dos Arcos used to be Lagoa do Desterro, drained in 1643. Lagoa do Boqueirão da Ajuda, for its part, was filled in with earth from the nearby hill, Morro das Mangueiras, to build the Passeio Público (Public Promenade, see p. 120). A little further south, at the level of the current Largo do Machado, Lagoa da Carioca and the Catete river (see p. 136) were also filled in.

A huge flooded mangrove swamp used to border Saco de São Cristóvão, a long stretch of seashore from the current Praça XI to the level of the Novo Rio bus station and Santo Cristo neighbourhood (where Praia Formosa and Saco do Alferes were located until the early 20th century). This area started to be reclaimed during the colonial period: the aim was to clean up the sites and facilitate movement between Palácio de São Cristóvão and Paço Real (nowadays known as Paço Imperial) on Praça XV. As the area to be filled in was considerable and the work costly, only a narrow route was made for the carriages of the imperial court. The drainage ditch running along the so-called Caminho do Aterrado (Terraced Path) was converted into a canal (Canal do Mangue) in the 16th century. In the early 20th century, during the construction of the new port of Rio, the canal was extended as far as the shore.

In a bid to modernise the city and mark the beginning of the Republic, the 20th century began under the sign of great urban projects. In the centre, the beaches of Dom Manuel and Peixe (now Praça XV) disappeared. Prainha (a small beach), on the site of what is now Praça Mauá, along with Saúde and Gamboa beaches, were covered by the foundations of the new port. The earth used for this landfill came from Morro do Senado, the hill having made way for Praça da Cruz Vermelha.

In 1922, with the levelling of Morro do Castelo (see p. 61), the beaches of Santa Luzia (Castelo), Ajuda (Cinelândia), Glória, Russel and Boqueirão (opposite the Passeio Público, see p. 120) as far as Calabouço (near the National Historical Museum) were filled in. This land reclaimed from the sea joined that of Avenida Beira-Mar (opened in 1906) and ran from the Obelisk to the end of the present Avenida Rio Branco, as far as Botafogo.

In the early 1950s, Aterro do Flamengo (reclaimed from the sea) was constructed thanks to the partial destruction of Morro de Santo Antônio.

In the place where the hill used to rise, there are new avenues with large buildings and the Cathedral of St Sebastian.

Part of Copacabana beach, in the Zona Sul, was built over in the 1970s in order to extend Avenida Atlantica. As for Lagoa Rodrigues de Freitas, over the years it has lost almost 40 per cent of its surface to sports clubs and residential buildings (built legally or illegally).

This urban policy hasn't been restricted to downtown Rio and the Zona Sul. In the Zona Norte, for example, the area from Point do Caju to Praia de Maria Angu is now covered with the *favelas* of Maré neighbourhood (see p. 306) and part of Avenida Brasil and Linha Vermelha. The archipelago that used to jut out near Enseada de Inhaúma has been integrated with Fundão island, home to the Universidade Federal do Rio de Janeiro campus.

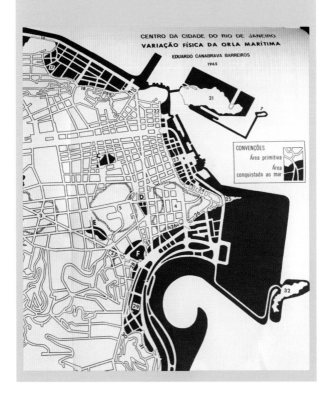

ART DECO DETAILS OF THE TRIBUNAL REGIONAL DO TRABALHO

⓵

105 Avenida Presidente Antônio Carlos, Centro
• Metro: Carioca

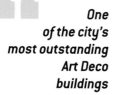

One of the city's most outstanding Art Deco buildings

The former Ministry of Labour, now the Regional Labour Court, is one of Rio's most striking buildings with its futuristic, sleek, New-York-skyscraper style and high-quality Art Deco ironwork.

The building, designed in 1936 by architect Mario Santos Maia (in collaboration with Affonso Eduardo Reidy, responsible for the Museu de Arte Moderna in the 1950s), features doors, gates and wrought-iron windows made in the workshops of Pellegrino and Fernandes, master ironworkers.

The interior aesthetic evokes the Bauhaus style, dominated by economical, austere solutions: the stairways and handrails are of chrome steel and the walls are glass brick, giving a truly streamlined look.

THE RAZING OF MORRO DO CASTELO TO MAKE WAY FOR ESPLANADA CASTELO AND ONE OF RIO'S CENTRES OF ART DECO

After Morro do Castelo (Castle hill) was demolished in the 1920s, the question arose of what to do with the site, which came to be known as Esplanada Castelo (Castle Esplanade). Although it lay empty for some years, part of it was used by the 1922 exposition commemorating the centenary of Brazil's independence (see p. 54). Once the pavilions had been dismantled (with a few exceptions, such as the French pavilion – see p. 55), doubts persisted: what to do with this huge area in the centre of Rio? On taking power in 1930, Getúlio Vargas, the "permanent president" (a euphemism used by North Americans to refer to the dictator), soon found a new use for the site, imagining it as a federal capital. Hence the city's largest concentration of Art Deco buildings: the ministries, courts and administrations of all sectors were housed in new, modern buildings, indicative of the global power that Brazil had become. A "New Brazil" exhibition was even inaugurated in 1938, showcasing models of completed buildings and others that were still at the planning stage.

CERAMICS AT THE MINISTÉRIO DA FAZENDA ㉕

Museu da Fazenda Federal
375 Avenida Presidente Antônio Carlos
• Guided tours (Portuguese only), Monday to Friday 9am—4pm. To book, call (21) 3805-2003 / 3805-2004
• Admission free
• Metro: Cinelândia

Works of art on the top floor of a ministry building

Very few Cariocas know that the terrace of the Ministry of Finance, on the 14th floor, hides a real gem of Brazilian modern art: panels by artist and muralist Paulo Werneck (1907.–1987) that incorporate ceramic mosaics.

Luiz Moura, the architect responsible for implementing the Ministry of Finance project, actually preferred more conservative designs. He surprised everyone by commissioning Werneck for these five ceramic panels inspired by indigenous culture and tropical nature: "You're part of the modern trend but you can draw," he said. "You're going to design the ministry's mosaics. The theme is up to you."

Werneck, widely considered to be Brazil's greatest 20th-century mosaic maker, was the first to work from live models. Years later, he described part of his work in these words: "The Indian man was based on a brave in the service of the Jesuits who defended their missions; he was called Sepé Tiaraju. The Indian woman, I don't remember. One of the panels depicts the Amazon, we see a toucan. On another, we have wild ducks, a lot of water, palm trees ..."

This was the first time that Werneck had worked in ceramics, thanks to the cooperation of Jorge Ludolf, regarded as the country's largest ceramics manufacturer at the time. The factory produced a wide variety of colours, "with totally stable materials and colours that are no longer made", Werneck claimed.

A VIEWPOINT THAT THROWS LIGHT ON MORRO DO CASTELO

The terrace doesn't only have a wonderful view, it's one of the best places to appreciate the site of the historic Morro do Castelo (see p. 61). This was levelled to make way for the present esplanade and the Ministries of Finance, Labour, Education and Health, among other buildings. The earth excavated from the hill was used to reclaim land from the sea, including the former beach in front of the Igrega de Santa Luzia, the church on the seashore where part of the Independence Centenary International Exposition was held in 1922 (see p. 54).

The terrace also features two glazed ceramic sculptures, again on an indigenous theme, by the artist Leão Velloso (1899–1966).
The Ministry of Finance also boasts a magnificent interior staircase (see following double-page spread).

STAIRWAY OF THE FORMER MINISTRY OF FINANCE

Palácio da Fazenda
375 Avenida Presidente Antônio Carlos, Castelo
• Guided tours (in Portuguese) Monday to Friday 9am–4pm (reservations by phone at (21) 3805-2003 / 3805-2004)
• Admission free
• Metro: Cinelândia

> *A spectacular and little-known flight of stairs*

As you enter the elevator lobby of Palácio da Fazenda (former Ministry of Finance), you'll immediately notice an imposing double flight of stairs. Two large chandeliers seem to float over the wide stairwells, of extreme lightness of touch despite their marble steps and gilded metal guardrails. From the first floor, the two flights meet and form just one spectacular spiral staircase, as you'll see during the guided tour. The railings are the work of Oreste Fabbro, who also designed the entrance doors and the decorative grilles at the counters.

The building, inaugurated in 1943, was the Ministry of Finance headquarters until Brasilia became the capital city in the early 1960s. Construction work began amid some controversy. The modernist project proposed by Wladimir Alves de Souza and Eneas Silva, winners of the architectural tender, was dismissed by the Minister of Finance, Arthur de Souza Costa (1893–1957), who preferred a neoclassical style. Such was his influence that he presented the project team with a photo of an Italian neoclassical building, declaring (even though plans for the new building were ready): "This is how I want the façade to look."

As part of the modernisation of Rio de Janeiro undertaken by the Getúlio Vargas government (see p. 128), two buildings were completed around the same time in hugely different styles: the neoclassical Palácio da Fazenda and the Ministry of Education and Health (Capanema – see p. 51), one of the main symbols of Brazilian modernism.

Palácio da Fazenda also features pretty modernist ceramics on the 14th floor (see following double-page spread).

Originally, the Ministry of Finance was to be built on Avenida Passos, near Praça Tiradentes, hence the demolition of the Imperial Academy of Fine Arts, designed by French architect Grandjean de Montigny and inaugurated in 1826. Only its entrance portico has been preserved: it is now at the Botanical Garden (see p. 120). On the site of the building, an infinitely sad parking lot struggles to forget its predecessor in the heart of the city.

IGREJA DE NOSSA SENHORA DO BONSUCESSO ㉗

206 Rua Santa Luzia
Centro
• Open Monday to Friday 9am–6.30pm
• Metro: Cinelândia

> *Memories of a prolonged miracle*

An antique table in the sacristy of the church of Our Lady of Good Success (the entrance is on Rua Santa Luzia – the main doorway is almost always closed) recalls a miracle that lasted an hour and a half and has lingered in people's memories for almost four centuries.

In 1637, Father Miguel Costa arrived in town with the first image of "Bom Sucesso", the original saint worshipped in Brazil, and obtained permission to install it on the altar at the Igreja da Misericórdia (Church of Mercy). The saint's feast day was always on the first Sunday after 8 September. The miracle took place at the first celebration: *"In the year 1639, on 11 September, during the Sunday in the octave of the nativity of the saint, the day when the first feast of Our Lady of Good Success was celebrated, at the introduction of the Holy Sacrament, the Virgin appeared in the form in which she is painted; she was seen by three priests over a period of an hour and a half and this miracle has been recognised."*

For an hour and a half, each worshipper taking communion actually saw the image of the Virgin, as explained by the text and the icon, which you can still see today. According to Brother Miguel de São Francisco, the miracle was repeated shortly afterwards when a novena (prayers repeated for nine consecutive days) was celebrated to alleviate the drought that was devastating the city. The saint's popularity grew to the point where she was considered patron of the Santa Casa hospital.

NEARBY

THE EYES OF THE CLOCK

In the same sacristy, almost directly opposite the image of the miraculous Virgin, a remarkable clock often goes unnoticed.

Yet stop a moment to look closely at it and you'll realise that the eyes of the chubby, friendly face inside, above the dial itself, accompany the swing of the pendulum.

A glance to the right, a glance to the left, as if this character was watching the passage of time …

ESTAÇÃO DE HIDROAVIÕES STAIRCASE

Instituto Histórico-Cultural da Aeronáutica (INCAER)
15-A Praça Marechal Âncora
Centro (next to Club da Aeronáutica)
• Open Monday to Friday 8.30am–12 noon (call to confirm summer schedule)
• Admission free
• Tel: (21) 2101-4966 / 2101-4967 • www.incaer.aer.mil.br
• Metro: Cinelândia

The Seaplane Station is still at Santos Dumont Airport

Although no longer operating, the Seaplane Station at Santos Dumont Airport, one of the icons of Brazilian modernist architecture, still exists. Its most interesting feature is probably the elegant concrete spiral staircase, rising 5.4 m between ground and first floor.

The building, with its spare and simple lines, has free-standing façades with a large expanse of glass that originally allowed a clear view of the city on one side and Guanabara bay on the other. Le Corbusier's five points of modern architecture feature in this project: supporting walls replaced by reinforced concrete columns (pilotis); free design of ground plan; free façade (separated from structural function); horizontal ribbon windows; and terrace or roof garden encouraging integration with the landscape.

The building, listed as historic and artistic national heritage in 1957, has suffered over time. The windows are now coated with a dark film to cut the glare of the tropical sun and reduce the heat inside. By the same token, the great hall on the ground floor – the former departure lounge – has been converted into a conference room. The first floor, which used to be a pleasant waiting area with overstuffed chairs, restaurant and bar, has become a storage space, although the outstanding aluminium-coated bar counter is still there. Also on the first floor, a terrace offers a fine view of Ilha Fiscal (Fiscal Island in Guanabara bay, where the border guards used to operate). From here you can also glimpse the original little spiral staircase leading to the garden and the covered walkway for boarding the seaplanes, now part of the Aerospace Club (private).

The Seaplane Station, opened in 1938, was designed by architect Attilio Corrêa Lima, winner of the previous year's architectural tenders. As aviation technology advanced, the station closed in 1942 and was temporarily ceded to the Aeronautical Club. Since 1986 INCAER has taken over the building. Corrêa Lima was killed nearby in 1943 when his plane crash-landed at Santos Dumont Airport.

The INCAER library has some 8,000 Brazilian and foreign aeronautical books, some of them rare or early editions.

OVAL PANELS BY LEANDRO JOAQUIM

Museu Histórico Nacional
Praça Marechal Âncora (next to Praça XV)
• Tel: (21) 3299-0300 / 3299-0324
• www.museuhistoriconacional.com.br
• Tuesday to Friday 10am–5.30pm; Saturdays, Sundays and public
holidays 2pm–6pm; closed Mondays
• Admission R$8, free Sundays
• Metro: Cinelândia, then about twenty minutes' walk

> **The only known painting of whaling in Guanabara bay**

The oval panels by Brazilian artist Leandro Joaquim (dating from around 1738–1798), on show at the National Historical Museum, are a rare depiction of 18th-century Rio and Guanabara bay. They are a visual chronicle of various aspects of daily life, different types of people and architectural details of the time. The works also illustrate the importance of the sea to the city – four of them are seascapes and the other two landscapes, although set by the sea.

The pictures are: *Vista da Igrega da Glória* (View from the Church of Glória), with the church that stands there today on the beach, since landfilled (see p. 131), and fishermen hauling a net; *Vista da Lagoa do Boqueirão e dos Arcos da Carioca* (View from the Lagoon of Boqueirão and the Arches of Carioca), which shows the Lapa Arches and Cariocas going about their business before the lagoon was filled in to form the Passeio Público (see p. 120), and in the foreground, a wave breaking on the beach; *Procissão ou romarío maritima ao Hospital dos Lázaros* (Procession or Maritime Pilgrimage to the Leprosarium), showing the hospital that still exists and a procession of boats at the beach of São Cristóvão, backfilled long ago; *Revista militar no Largo do Paço* (Military Review in the Largo do Paco), which proves that what is now Praça XV has many 18th-century elements – Paço Imperial (Imperial Palace), then the viceroy's residence, the churches of Carmo (Carmel) and the Third Order of Carmelites, the Arch of Teles and, on what was the dockside, the Fountain of Mestre Valentim; *Cena marítima* (Maritime Scene), showing a visiting British squadron anchored alongside Villegagnon fortress, now the Naval Academy; and finally, *Pesca da baleia na Baía de Guanabara* (Whaling in the Bay of Guanabara), the only known painting of everyday fishing in the bay during the 18th century.

The panels (eight originally, but two have been lost) were commissioned to decorate the pavilions of the Passeio Público terraces, and are among the country's first sea and landscape paintings by a Brazilian artist.

SUGAR LOAVES AT THE NATIONAL HISTORICAL ③⓪ MUSEUM

Museu Histórico Nacional
Praça Marechal Âncora (next to Praça XV)
• Tel: (21) 3299-0300 / 3299-0324
• www.museuhistoriconacional.com.br
• Tuesday to Friday 10am–5.30pm; Saturdays, Sundays and public holidays 2pm–6pm; closed Mondays • Admission R$8, free Sundays
• Metro: Cinelândia, then about twenty minutes' walk

An example of what gave its name to the famous Sugar Loaf

For those who have never really understood the origin of the name "sugar loaf", Rio's National Historical Museum has had the brilliant idea of including two real sugar loaves in its collection.

As found in the museum, a sugar loaf is a conical block of sugar (the same shape as Urca's famous Sugarloaf Mountain and the cones used for refining sugar).

This is the form in which loaf sugar was sold until the late 19th century, when it was gradually replaced by granulated or cube sugar, although loaf is still used in some traditional societies. The great advantage of the loaf shape is that it keeps really well: it resists the ravages of time, unlike other forms of packaging such as those used for granulated or cubed sugar. Loaf sugar can be transported over long distances with little risk of damage, hence its success in remote and inaccessible regions and impoverished regions where price is all-important.

The technical processes of sugar manufacturing have determined its conical shape: the loaf mould, made from earthenware, metal or wood, consisted of a relatively wide base rising in a conical shape with a hole at the end. The inverted mould (hole at the bottom) was filled with sugar-cane juice and the top covered with a layer of clay. Every day, for 30 to 40 days, water was poured

into the mould through the sugar-cane juice, to drain out of the hole at the bottom.

At the end of this filtration process, the whitest, most refined sugar was at the top of the loaf, the darkest at the bottom.

LIBRARY OF THE MUSEU HISTÓRICO NACIONAL ③

Praça Marechal Âncora (near Praça XV)
• Library open Monday to Friday 2pm–5pm
• Tel: (21) 3299-0351
• E-mail: mhn.biblioteca@museus.gov.br
• www.museuhistoriconacional.com.br

A forgotten library

Few visitors to the National Historical Museum realise that it also has a library. There is a good reason for this: in order to find it, visitors have to go through the main entrance and up to the first floor, and, instead of visiting the first room on the right, take the door leading to the museum's small terrace. This leads to the library which, in addition to its book collections (all available for consultation), has beautiful painted ceilings by Carlos Oswald (1882–1971), who also decorated the Large Industries Pavilion at the 1922 International Exposition. The library now occupies part of the original pavilion building (see p. 55).

BAS-RELIEFS AT THE CENTRO ADMINISTRATIVO DO TRIBUNAL DE JUSTIÇA

②

2 Praça XV de Novembro
Centro

*Art Deco
in Praça XV*

Designed in 1941 by architect Humberto Nabuco dos Santos, the Administrative Centre of the Court of Justice, in Praça XV, features some remarkable Art Deco bas-reliefs whose existence is unknown to many Cariocas.

The sculptures by Armando Sócrates Schnoor, set on top of two U-shaped columns at the entrance to the building, depict men from Brazil's different ethnic groups engaged in fishing.

The building previously housed the federal fishing warehouse and the Companhia Nacional de Abastecimento (CONAB), the National Supply Company.

STROLL DOWN THE RUNWAY AT AEROPORTO DO SANTOS DUMONT ③③

Avenida Almirante Silvio de Noronha
• Bus: 2018, towards the airport; all buses through Parque do Flamengo, near the airport

> **Watch planes taking off at very close quarters**

If you drive to Santos Dumont Airport, follow the route signposted "Escola Naval" that skirts the airport. After about 100 m, another sign indicates that the end of the airport's only runway is still nearly 300 m away. If you manage to follow the acoustic signals and signs on Avenida Almirante Silvio de Noronha, which crosses the end of the track, you'll have earned a lovely walk (with a novel view of Sugarloaf Mountain, Christ the Redeemer, the Rio-Niterói bridge and the far side of the bay), but above all a real adrenaline burst.

The road passes just a few metres from the end of the runway, with aircraft taking off and landing all the time. If you strictly follow the signage (*não insista* – don't insist – as road signs in Brazil often read), you'll experience a hair-raising spectacle: a few metres away from the aircraft taking off, the engine noise is really deafening. Although along the road to the Naval Academy on the neighbouring island of Villegagnon (linked by a bridge), you'll only have seen planes landing, in the other direction the effect is more spectacular. You'll be startled by the din of the engines as planes take off behind you and pass just overhead.

No worries if you're impatient: the traffic is intense, and a plane lands or takes off every two to three minutes on average

Despite what you might think, Avenida Almirante Silvio de Noronha is a public highway without traffic restrictions. There are no buses, only cars, taxis, bikes and pedestrians. If you have time to spare before your flight, the beginning of the runway, via the avenue, is just a five-minute walk from the departure terminal.

This is also a meeting place for plane spotters, of course.

The earth from the excavation of Morro do Castelo (see p. 61), and later Morro de Santo Antônio, was used as landfill for Santos Dumont Airport runway (1,350 m long) when it was reclaimed from the ocean.

A PLANE THAT OVERTURNED A TAXI

This place is a danger spot, as pointed out in an interview with Jorge Barros, aviation safety expert: "People don't realise the destructive power of the blast from a turbine. It can overturn a truck and roll it over several times. In 2002, the air movement caused by a plane's engines at take-off overturned a taxi on Avenida Silvio de Noronha. The driver was thrown out of his vehicle and killed." According to the news reports, he had apparently ignored the signals on the avenue.

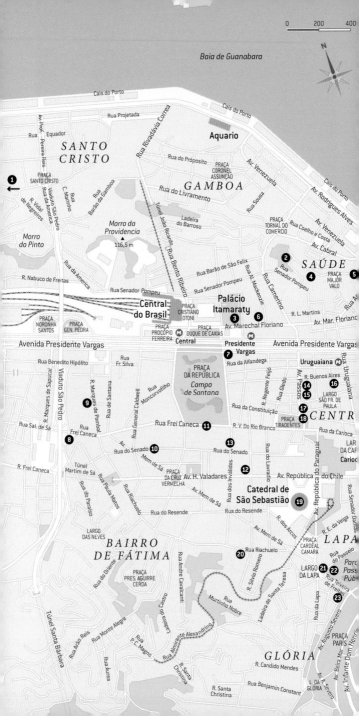

LAPA - CENTRO
GAMBOA - SAÚDE

RARE NEO-EGYPTIAN BUILDING ❶

40 / 42 Rua Pedro Alves
Taxi recommended

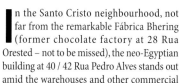

*Egyptian
allegories*

I n the Santo Cristo neighbourhood, not far from the remarkable Fábrica Bhering (former chocolate factory at 28 Rua Orested – not to be missed), the neo-Egyptian building at 40 / 42 Rua Pedro Alves stands out amid the warehouses and other commercial or industrial buildings.

The 1910 construction is one of the city's most stunningly beautiful architectural achievements, and still in perfect condition.

The variety of its decoration is particularly striking, with original versions of symbols such as palm-shaped capitals, the rising Sun (allegory of the god Ra), falcon wings (allegory of the god Horus) and winged scarabs (symbol of the rebirth of the soul).

There is another neo-Egyptian building in downtown Rio (see p. 37).

Although the worldwide fashion for Egyptian-style buildings developed after Napoleon Bonaparte's Egyptian campaign of 1798, he actually only followed a trend already well established in Europe. From the mid-18th century, young artists went to Italy to seek the Etruscan and Egyptian origins of Roman art. At the time of the French Revolution, which was heavily influenced by Freemasonry, there already was a lively interest in the cult of the dead and the mysteries of Egyptian art dear to the Freemasons.

OBSERVATÓRIO DO VALONGO ❷

43 Ladeira do Pedro Antônio
Centro
• Open: Mon-Fri 9am–4pm
• Observations on the first and third Wednesdays of each month at 6.30pm (presentation of an astronomical theme at 6pm)
• Observations of the Sun, with filter, several times a year
• Free entry
• Tel: (21) 2263-0685 • ov@astro.ufrj.br • www.ov.ufrj.br

Observe the stars, Sun and Moon from the city centre

Valongo Observatory, the astronomical observatory of the UFRJ, is less well known than Brazil's National Observatory at São Cristóvão. On the heights of Morro da Conceição, it's easily accessible directly from Ladeira do Pedro Antônio, overlooking Rua da Conceição. Twice a month the observatory invites the public along to observe the stars.

After a half-hour presentation on an astronomical topic (during our visit, 'stellar winds – source of the *Aurora Borealis*'), you move straight to the telescopes (there's usually one set up on the lawn in front of the main building). The atmosphere is relaxed, far from the crowds that frequent São Cristóvão. Depending on the timing of your visit, you'll see Mercury, Saturn and its rings and, of course, the truly spectacular Moon - on good days you can even make out the contours of the craters on its surface. The experience is totally unmissable.

In addition to the outdoor telescope, the Coudé telescope under its pretty wooden dome lets you observe Saturn in detail. Although you may get a better picture of the planet online, seeing it 'for real' through the telescope is something special.

On weekdays you can visit the observatory itself, whose main attraction is the Cooke & Sons telescope under a beautiful antique dome in the main building.

Valongo Observatory owes its existence to Manoel Pereira Reis (1837–1922). He fell out with Emmanuel Liais (1826–1900), the French director of the Observatório Imperial, where Pereira Reis worked as an astronomer. In association with Joaquim Galdino Pimentel and André Gustavo Paulo de Frontin, he acquired land on Morro de Santo Antônio, near the Escola Politécnica, where they built and gradually developed a small observatory.

The destruction of Morro de Santo Antônio (see following double-page spread) and Morro do Castelo (then home to the Imperial Observatory) in the 1920s was an incentive to transfer the observatory to its present location between 1924 and 1926. The main entrance and the buildings that house the domes for the Cooke and Pazos telescopes were reconstructed in an almost identical style to the Santo Antônio buildings.

MUSEU HISTÓRICO E DIPLOMÁTICO OF THE PALÁCIO ITAMARATY

❸

196 Avenida Marechal Floriano
• Visits by appointment only
• Tel: (21) 2253-2828
• Email: ererio.museu@itamaraty.gov.br
• To visit the library Monday to Friday 10am–5pm, phone (21) 2253-5720

A forgotten jewel

By appointment only (see above), it is possible to visit the Historic and Diplomatic Museum in the Itamaraty Palace, headquarters of the Ministry of Foreign Affairs between 1899 and 1970.

In addition to the collections (paintings, furniture, decorations and objects associated with the history of Brazilian diplomacy), visitors can see the remarkable rooms that now house the museum: the Indian salon with its magnificent indigenous-style wallpaper (unfortunately in bad condition) as well as the ballroom and the former office of the Baron of Rio Branco, Minister of Foreign Affairs between 1902 and 1912. He played a crucial role in Brazilian political life. It was his diplomatic skill in particular that resolved the border disputes with Argentina, France (the frontier with French Guiana) and, most notably, Bolivia. In 1903, he negotiated the transfer of the state of Acre from Bolivia to Brazil. Rio Branco, the state capital, was named after him.

Visitors to the museum can go out onto a terrace with a lovely view over the historic library, ornamental lake and stately palm trees located within the inner garden. The palace owes its existence to Francisco José da Rocha (1806–1883), Count of Itamaraty, a wealthy trader in coffee and precious stones. He commissioned José Maria Jacinto Rebelo, a disciple of Grandjean de Montigny, to build the palace in 1854.

In 1889, the house was sold to the Republic of Brazil, which made it the headquarters of the presidency before it was used as the Ministry of Foreign Affairs.

THE HISTORIC LIBRARY

After the creation of Avenida Presidente Vargas, a decision was taken to construct a new building for the library. It was designed between 1927 and 1930 by the Scottish architect Robert Prentice (also responsible for the Leopoldina railway station, see p. 279) and his Austrian colleague Anton Floderer (who designed the Lacerda Elevator, in Salvador de Bahia).

No expense was spared: the windows and bronze doors came from England, the artificial ventilation and a paper disinfection machine were imported from Germany, while the linoleum flooring and a machine for refrigerating drinking water came from the United States.

Please note: entrance to the museum does not include access to the library. A separate reservation is required (see above).

PALÁCIO EPISCOPAL AND FORTALEZA DA CONCEIÇÃO

4

81 Rua Major Daemon
Saúde
• Open: Mon-Thur 8am–4pm, Friday 8am–12 noon
• Tel: (21) 2223-2177 for reservations
• www.5dl.eb.mil.br

A historical look at the city

The 5ª Divisão de Levantamento (5th Division of Topographic Surveys) has been installed since 1922 in unique premises in the heart of Morro da Conceição. Despite its central location, many Cariocas remain unfamiliar with this particular hill.

The buildings, listed in 1938, include the beautiful old Bishop's Palace with its charming cloister (built in 1702), and the former Fortress of the Immaculate Conception, established in 1713 as part of the city's defence system.

You can book a tour round the Museu Cartográfico do Serviço Geográfico do Exército (Army Cartographic Museum) in the palace; the library, located in what used to be a chapel; and the old fortress with its armoury where three conspirators were incarcerated during the Conjuração Mineira (Minas Gerais Conspiracy, see box) in 1791, including the celebrated Portuguese-born poet Tomás Antônio Gonzaga. Note that the armoury was built in 1765 to resemble a chapel with the aim of deceiving the enemy about the real function of the site, thus reducing the chances of being bombarded.

Although the museum with its displays of Brazilian mapmaking tools isn't particularly stimulating, the tour provides insight into the general charm of the place, its historical character and the lovely panoramic views over the city.

In 1905 Archbishop Arcoverde, in residence at the Bishop's Palace, was appointed as the first Latin American cardinal.

The palace itself stands over the remains of a small monastery built in 1669 by French Capuchin monks, who were expelled from Brazil in 1701. Previously (in 1655), a hermitage built on the site in 1634 had been ceded to the Carmelite order.

In 1923, after the new official residence of the Bishops of Rio (Palácio São Joaquim) was constructed at Glória in 1918, the Conceição palace, which had been standing empty, was bought by the army.

The Conjuração Mineira was an unsuccessful Brazilian separatist movement against the Portuguese colonisers that arose in 1789 in Minas Gerais. The rebellion was led by Tiradentes, who was denounced and captured in Rio on 10 May 1789.

RIO DE JANEIRO, THE WORLD'S LARGEST PORT OF ENTRY FOR SLAVES

It is estimated that half of all the African slaves deported to the American continent arrived via Brazil, which received about four million slaves over the three centuries in which slavery was practised in the country.

In the 19th century, the Valongo Wharf saw the transfer of between 500,000 and 1 million slaves, making it the largest port of entry for slaves in the world. Estimates suggest that until slavery was abolished, Rio alone received 20% of all the African slaves who reached the American continent alive. This makes the city and Valongo Wharf landmarks in what was the largest deportation in human history.

The Valongo Wharf, which forms part of the historical and archaeological tour celebrating the city's African heritage, "was built for receiving and marketing slaves. After the arrival of the Portuguese court in Rio, in 1808, this trade became inconvenient, as people were being sold in the street, dressed in pieces of cloth covering their crotches, people being sold like animals [...]", explains the historian of Africa, Alberto da Costa e Silva. Constructed in 1811, the wharf was closed in 1831 and altered to receive Teresa Cristina, Princess of the Two Sicilies, who later married Dom Pedro II. This is why it is also known as the Empress Wharf.

The wharf was backfilled in 1911 as part of the renovation work undertaken in the city. During excavations in the port area in 2011 and 2012, remains from the African slave period were discovered. "We found an extensive material culture belonging to the ruling classes and African slaves. The area was steeped in Black culture and became known as Little Africa" (a nickname given to it by the composer and samba player, Heitor dos Prazeres), according to archaeologist Tania Andrade Lima.

There are other sites in Rio that form part of the tour celebrating the city's African heritage: the **Hanging Garden of Valongo**, laid out at the beginning of the 20th century in order to wipe out all traces of the slave trade, located on the western side of the Conceição district on Rua do Camerino; the **Largo do Depósito**, present-day Praça dos Estivadores, at the entrance to Rua Barão de São Felix; the **Pedra do Sal** (Rock of Salt), Rua Argemiro Bulcão, at the foot of the Conceição district, a full-fledged monument to historical and religious tradition, where samba concerts are held every week; the **José Bonifácio Cultural Centre**, at 80 Rua Pedro Ernesto, an outreach and exploration centre for Black culture, housed in a (now completely restored) building, opened in 1876 by Dom Pedro II as the first public (state) school in Latin America; and the **Pretos Novos Cemetery** (Cemetery of the New Blacks), at 36 Rua Pedro Ernesto, discovered by accident in 1996, which holds the remains of Blacks from Africa who died before they could be sold.

"THESE ARE HUMAN REMAINS!"

In 1996, Merced Guimarães, Director of the "Pretos Novos" Institute (see opposite), unearthed a genuine archaeological site buried in his house: "The house needed work. On the first day, the builder came and said that the previous owners must have had a lot of dogs, as the ground was full of bones. I took a jawbone and noticed that it did not come from a dog but was a human bone! The police then visited, along with the archaeologists, and they decided that this was the location of the Pretos Novos Cemetery."

"FOR THE ENGLISH TO SEE…"

In 1831, the Valongo Wharf was closed following the banning of the transatlantic slave trade, under pressure from Great Britain. The regulation was arrogantly ignored, however, and became known ironically as the "Para inglês ver" law ("For the English to see"), an expression still used today to describe something that exists solely for the sake of appearances. The slave trade with Brazil was genuinely halted with the signing of the Eusébio de Queirós law in 1850, although the last known expedition dates from 1872 and slavery persisted until it was finally abolished in 1888.

Valongo Wharf was declared part of the national heritage in November 2013, when UNESCO determined that the site was part of the "Slave Route", a project inaugurated by the organisation in 2006 in order to highlight the tangible and intangible heritage of the global slave trade. In 2016, the UNESCO World Heritage Centre accepted Valongo Wharf's application to be categorised as world heritage.

Circulam pelas ladeiras do Morro da Conceição várias histórias. Uma delas conta que, quando o Edifício A Noite foi fechado pelo governo militar, as máquinas de escrever foram jogadas pelas janelas e emparedadas nos banheiros públicos que ficam no sopé do morro, na escadinha do Imaculada.

Alguns moradores aproveitaram a oportunidade e levaram máquinas para suas casas. Temos uma delas emprestada por um dos descendentes e contador de histórias.

IMACULADA BAR TYPEWRITER

7 Ladeira do João Homem
Morro da Conceição
• Open Monday to Saturday 11am–10pm
• Bus: 119, 177, 222
• Tel: (21) 2253-3999
• www.barimaculada.com.br

> *The day
> that typewriters
> flew out
> the windows*

In the friendly Imaculada bar, an old typewriter sits in a niche in the right-hand wall, near the stairs leading to the upper floor. Older locals recall that on 1 April 1964, following the military coup of 31 March and just as the marines were taking over Radio Nacional, typewriters were hurled out of the windows of the offices of the evening paper *A Noite*, near the present bar. Witnesses say that the journalists wanted to destroy the typewriters because the ribbons could have revealed what they'd been writing about. They fell right next to the staircase leading to the bar and some neighbours took them home. It's one of these machines, on loan from a neighbour, that is on display in the Imaculada bar.

Radio Nacional, founded in 1936 and nationalised in 1940 by the Federal Government, played an important role in Brazilian integration by transmitting throughout the territory. The largest broadcasting service in Latin America at that time, the station had access to plenty of extremely popular artists, launched the country's first radio soap, introduced innovative comedy programmes and pioneered modern radio journalism. The decline of Radio Nacional began with the advent of television; this decline became more marked after the military coup of 1964, which led to the dismissal of sixty-seven employees and subjected eighty-one others to an investigation.

A NOITE: THE TALLEST BUILDING IN LATIN AMERICA UNTIL 1934

Radio Nacional was (and still is) housed on the top floors of an icon of Brazilian architecture, opened in 1929 as the headquarters of the newspaper *A Noite*. The building at 7 Praça Mauá (twenty-two floors and 102 m high) is an Art Deco joint project by French architect Joseph Gire (who also designed Copacabana Palace and Palácio Laranjeiras) and Brazilian architect Elisário Bahiana. Its reinforced concrete design inspired many of the country's modern buildings. In 1934, with the inauguration of the Martinelli building in São Paulo (105 m), the *A Noite* building was no longer the tallest in Latin America.

For decades, it was the meeting point for Radio Nacional celebrities and regulars who frequented the restaurants and roof terrace. Until the Cristo Redentor (Christ the Redeemer) statue was completed at Corcovado in 1931, the top floor of the building was the main viewpoint over the city. In the 1970s the building became more and more dilapidated.

DI CAVALCANTI FRESCOES ON THE NEWSROOM ❻

Centro Cultural Light
168 Avenida Marechal Floriano - Centro
• Metro: Presidente Vargas
• Open: Mon-Fri 11am–5pm
• Free entry
• Tel: (21) 2211-4515 • Email: ccl@light.com.br

*Painting
for the visually
impaired*

In Rio's downtown Light Cultural Centre, four panels of a series of five by the celebrated modernist painter Di Cavalcanti, featuring the press at work, can be 'seen' by the visually impaired. Along with Portuguese and Braille captions that explain the artwork, there are bas-reliefs that let blind people understand the design of each panel by running their hands over small marble reproductions.

The main component of *Composition Rio* – as the entire work is known – is the reporter, represented by a man with two faces turned in opposite directions, intent on turning facts and figures into news. This duality is symbolized by the Sun and the Moon, expressing the pressure of time on the journalist's day. On these panels – restored to perfect condition – Di Cavalcanti's vibrant aesthetic sense and use of many colours capture the intense pace of the newsroom, underlining the importance of the press to society. He also showcases the diversity of information and people's reactions to it, the role of the law and the diversity of Brazilian culture.

The artist was commissioned for these panels by Samuel Wainer, founder and owner of the daily *Última hora* (At the Last Minute) based in Rio, to celebrate the newspaper's first anniversary in 1952. They were kept in the office until 1970 when Wainer, who was in financial difficulties, put them up for sale. Four of the panels were bought by Light. Displayed in various places over the years, they are now on permanent exhibition in a special room at the Light Cultural Center, opened in mid-2014. A photo of the fifth panel is also shown.

Emiliano Augusto Cavalcanti de Albuquerque e Melo (1897–1976), a major modernist painter, draftsman, illustrator and caricaturist, was the director of the Semana de Arte Moderna (Week of Modern Art) in 1922. A friend of Picasso, Matisse and Jean Cocteau, known as the 'Métis painter', Di Cavalcanti said: *I couldn't live without Rio de Janeiro, for everything that I see as a painter is part of the Carioca landscape.*

Última Hora was a benchmark in Brazilian journalism through its technical and graphic innovations. In the words of Samuel Wainer it was "a newspaper in opposition to the ruling class and in favour of a government" (that of Getúlio Vargas). Founded on 12 June 1951, it was sold to the *Folha de São Paulo* in 1971 and finally stopped publication in 1991.

SÃO DIMAS

STATUE OF SÃO DISMAS   ❼

Igreja de São Gonçalo Garcia e São Jorge
382 Rua da Alfândega
• Open Monday to Friday 7am–4.30pm, Saturday 7.30am–11.30am,
Sunday 8am–11am

*A rare
image of
the penitent thief
crucified
with Jesus*

To the right of the main entrance of the church dedicated to St Gonçalo Garcia and St George, the sharp-eyed visitor will spot the statue of a crucified man. Unlikely as it seems, this doesn't represent Christ: the name of São Dimas (St Dismas) is given at the foot of the cross.

Although his name doesn't appear in the New Testament canon, it does in the apocryphal Gospel of Nicodemus, the disciple who helped Joseph of Arimathea with the descent from the Cross and the entombment of Christ.

Dismas, whose feast day is celebrated on 12 October in the East and 25 March in the West, was the first saint in the Church's history, canonised for having converted on the cross just before dying. While Dismas, Christ and Gesmas (the impenitent thief, whose name also appears in the Gospel of Nicodemus) were already on the cross, Gesmas began to taunt Jesus: "Are you not the Christ? Save yourself and us."

Dismas then rebuked Gesmas: "Don't you fear God, since you are under the same sentence? We are punished justly, for we are getting what our deeds deserve: but this man has done nothing wrong." He added: "Jesus, remember me when you come into your Kingdom." Having repented of his

sins and recognised Jesus as the Saviour, Christ told him just before he died: "You will be with me in Paradise" (Luke 23:40–43).

Dismas is also traditionally mentioned during the flight to Egypt as one of two bandits who robbed the Holy Family of their money and their donkey. Moved by their poverty on the road to exile, Dismas returned their property. The Child Jesus thanked him, promising that he would remember him, which he did at the Crucifixion.

LAGARTO FOUNTAIN ON RUA FREI CANECA   **8**

Corner of Rua Frei Caneca and Rua Salvador de Sá

A forgotten lizard

At the point where Rua Frei Caneca crosses Rua Salvador de Sá and skirts the hill, opposite the police station on one side and the Sambódromo on the other, it's easy to miss the lizard at the centre of a niche that was part of the region's water supply.

The water gushing from the lizard's jaws was collected in a basin, now overgrown with plants that cover – and protect – the lizard. This isn't the original bronze, but a steel copy.

At the centre of the structure, an oval panel bears a Latin phrase: *sitienti populu – senatus profusit aquas – anno MDCCLXXXVI* ("to the thirsty people the senate gave abundant water in the year 1786"). The engraved inscription fails to mention the sculptor of the little reptile, which is attributed to Mestre Valentim (1745–1813).

Thanks to the lizard's capacity to regrow its tail, and because it hibernates, the reptile is associated with healing and resurrection, also linked to the waters of the fountain.

NEARBY

9

MUSEU DA POLÍCIA MILITAR DO ESTADO DO RIO DE JANEIRO
128 Rua Marques de Pombal
• Open Tuesday to Thursday 9am–4pm
• Admission free
• Tel: (21) 2332-6668 / 2242-4059

Two minutes' walk from the lizard fountain, the Military Police Museum, housed in a beautiful 19th-century mansion, has objects and documents relating to the history of Rio's police forces. Key exhibits include the armour collection from the 15th and 16th centuries brought over by the Portuguese crown in 1808, some antique weapons, and a room devoted to the Paraguay War complete with a stuffed dog that took part in the conflict.

FAÇADE OF THE FORMER LAMBERT PERFUME AND SOAP FACTORY

⑩

244–246 Rua do Senado
• Metro: Central

A stunning yet forgotten façade

Forgotten in Rua do Senado, the blue and white façade at number 244–246 is one of the most charming in the city and in very good condition. The first floor has a remarkable sculpture of a woman, holding a hammer resting on an anvil in her right hand, and in her left hand a set square and compass.

Built in 1920, the building once housed the former Lambert perfume and soap factory, as told by photographer and historian Luiz Eugênio Teixeira Leite in his extraordinary book, *O Rio que o Rio não vê* (The Rio that Rio Doesn't See). In one sense, the hammer and anvil refer to the former industrial activity (production of consumer goods). The square and compass, which on the face of it, symbolise the architect's work, are also Masonic symbols.

For Freemasons, the compass symbolises the Spirit, whereas the square (symbol of Matter) indicates "righteousness in action". When both tools are linked, they express the balance between spiritual and material forces, a necessary condition to achieve spiritual enlightenment. This enlightenment is represented in the Masonic hierarchy by the 3rd grade of Master Mason, where the compass is placed *on* the square (as here), indicating that spirituality has *conquered* matter.

Is this the meaning of the laurel crown (symbol of victory) on the statue's head?

Similarly, the large shell carved above the woman is often, by its very form, associated with the female sexual organ. Its presence would also recall the victory of the spirit over human sexual (material) instincts.

MUSEU DE BOMBEIROS

45 Praça da República
Centro
Open Tuesday to Friday 9am–5pm

> *Stories of the Rio firefighters*

The Firefighters Museum (full name: Museu Histórico do Corpo de Bombeiros Militar do Estado do Rio de Janeiro), established in 1977, is of interest on two counts. On the one hand, it shows a history of firefighting since the service was established by Emperor Dom Pedro II in 1856. But it also admits visitors to the monumental fire station in Praça da República to experience something of its working atmosphere, as well as offering a closer look at the climbing wall used for training purposes at the back of the main yard.

The museum itself, housed in a beautiful glass and steel building, has displays of model fire trucks, a selection of helmets, and accounts from the history of fighting Rio fires.

You'll discover that there used to be several ways of sounding a fire alarm: a cannon fired from Morro do Castelo (now gone to landfill, see p. 61); the church bells of the particular parish where a fire had been spotted; and the church bells of São Francisco de Paula. In 1879/1880, however, twelve fire hydrants were installed in the city centre – they were supposed to be operated by the first person to discover a fire.

The Praça da República fire station was built in 1908 to the plans of Marshal Francisco Marcelino de Souza Aguiar.

NEARBY

The musical notes on the pavement near the entrance to the right of the fire station correspond to the firefighters' anthem.

MUSEU DA POLÍCIA CIVIL WAXWORKS

40 Rua da Relação
• Open Monday to Friday 10.30am–5pm
• www.policiacivil.rj.gov.br/museu/museo1.htm

Museum open despite renovations

The Civil Police Museum isn't closed to the public, despite the endless work being carried out in the superb main building, dating from 1910. However, not all the historical collection is on display, as objects associated with spiritualist cults or Candomblé are in storage.

In addition to weapons and uniforms, the exhibits include some notable fake documents as well as Dr Alberto Baldissara's impressive wax reproductions of faces and body parts. The idea was to preserve the traces of violent crimes as realistically as possible, to help the forensic teams.

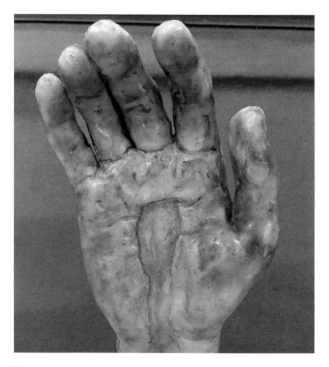

RIGHT ARM OF NOSSA SENHORA DOS PRAZERES' STATUE

⑬

Igreja de Santo Antônio dos Pobres
42 Rua dos Inválidos, Centro (corner of Rua do Senado)
• Tel: (21) 2222-2586
• Open Monday to Friday 7.30am–5pm, Saturday 7.30am–12 noon, Sunday 7am–12 noon
• Admission free
• Bus: 126, 161, 201, 433, 464

A saint persecuted by thieves

The first side altar to the right as you enter the church of St Anthony of the Poor is dedicated to Nossa Senhora dos Prazeres (Our Lady of the Pleasures). Her statue used to stand in the oratory bearing her name at Arco do Teles, Praça XV de Novembro, in the 18th century. Around 1830 it was moved here by a believer, Manoel Machado de Oliveira, to save it from the alcoholics, thieves and vandals who frequented the area around "Praça Quinze", as the square is generally known.

Somewhat ironically, in 2013 a thief up to his usual tricks broke the stained-glass window behind the small altar and snapped off the statue's right arm as he clambered into the church. The statue was repaired but the restored arm has been left unpainted as a reminder of this lamentable deed, as any keen-eyed visitor will notice. Moreover, the replacement glass is completely at odds with the rest of the window.

The original Baroque church was consecrated in 1811. In 1831, as the church had grown too small and was in a poor state of repair, another was built

in the same style. This was restored in 1854, using slaked lime and concrete slabs for the flooring. But the constant floods in the area damaged the foundations and walls, which is why a new church – the third – was built at the same location between 1940 and 1949 in a neo-Romanesque style. The stained-glass windows depicting the life of St Anthony are installed 1.20 m above street level to prevent flooding.

RAISED FLOOR OF IGREJA DO SANTÍSSIMO SACRAMENTO DA ANTIGA SÉ ⓮

50 Avenida Passos
• Open Monday to Friday 8am—4.30pm, Sunday 8.30am—2pm

> *Short slaves in their place at Mass*

Entering the church of the Holy Sacrament of the Old Cathedral, you don't immediately spot the slightly raised section (measuring over 3 or 4 m) of the 19th-century tiled flooring in the nave.

Despite what you might think, nobody's buried beneath the floor. This area was purposely raised so that the shorter slaves (those below 1.6 m) could stand and watch Mass being celebrated. The taller slaves had to stand at the back.

As this church was consecrated in 1859, and slavery wasn't abolished until the Lei Áurea (Golden Law) of 1888, it was of its time: the slaves stood at the back. Seated in front were the bourgeoisie and merchants, then on the left the *fazendeiros* (farmers) and on the right religious brotherhoods, such as the Santíssimo Sacramento da Antiga Sé, founded between 1567 and 1569, which built this church.

Note that the last three rows of the farmers' pews have a small but significant detail – engraved at the entrance to each is an "X", two "Xs" or three "Xs", depending on the wealth of their *fazendas*. The brotherhoods' pews are

likewise engraved with the Roman numerals I, II and III, signifying their degree of affluence.

The nobility took part in Mass from the first floor, seated in the lodges that can still be seen on either side of the choir.

The church also boasts the oldest baptismal font in Rio. Down at the far right, don't miss the charming chapel of Nossa Senhora da Piedade (Our Lady of Piety), where the ceiling is unfortunately disintegrating.

CASA FRANKLIN FAÇADE

36 Avenida Passos
Centro

A
hundred-year-old
peacock

Number 36 Avenida Passos, just a few steps from the Igreja de Santíssimo Sacramento da Antiga Sé (Church of the Holy Sacrament of the Old Cathedral), is one of the city's architectural gems. But in a busy street with relatively narrow sidewalks it's easy to walk past this 1911 building without even noticing it. The spectacular façade features thirteen French stained-glass windows that form a large peacock's tail. Each "feather" bears a letter which, when combined, spell the name Casa Franklin. This intricate façade, with its Art Nouveau elements, is topped by a bronze eagle holding a lamp in its beak. The building, which was originally an electrical and hardware store, can now be hired as a venue for large functions and parties.

NEARBY

MUSEU DA BÍBLIA

135 Rua Buenos Aires
• Open Monday to Friday 9am–6pm

On the first floor of a religious book store, a canopy-covered space houses a small museum dedicated to the Bible. There are some interesting explanations about the origins of the Bible and the fact that it has been translated into more than 2,300 languages (the museum has a copy in Guaraní and one in Tupana Ehay, the language of an Indian tribe from northern Brazil). Other unusual items include a stone from Mount Sinai, two containers of water from the Dead Sea, and especially (children love this) perfumes from biblical times that you can smell, like the Magi's famous myrrh.

DI CAVALCANTI PANELS AT THE JOÃO CAETANO THEATRE

17

Teatro João Caetano
Praça Tiradentes
• Metro: Carioca
• Open during performances

> *Brazil's first two modernist paintings*

The first-floor foyer of the João Caetano Theatre – originally built in 1813 and extensively renovated over the following two centuries – is the hiding place of two valuable panels by Di Cavalcanti painted in oil on mortarboard, dating from 1929.

These paintings, entitled *Samba* and *Carnaval*, are barely known to Cariocas: the foyer behind the first-floor balcony is little used, despite the posters tracing the history of the theatre and the fact that visitors have to pass through there to find the toilets.

The paintings themselves have been restored a number of times, most recently in 1995.

Strongly influenced by Mexican muralists José Clemente Orozco and David Alfaro Siqueiros, the panels depict mixed-race characters dancing the samba to the sound of the flute, *pandeiro* (a kind of tambourine), tambourine, guitar and *cavaquinho* (a small guitar). These are probably Brazil's first two modernist paintings. From the 1920s, this movement sought to go back to the Brazilian roots of music, literature and the arts in general.

This decade was a fertile period that saw the emergence of Emiliano Di Cavalcanti, Cândido Portinari and Tarsila (do Amaral) in the visual arts, poets Carlos Drummond de Andrade and Manuel Bandeira, and writers Jorge Amado, Graciliano Ramos and Raquel de Queiroz, as well as the music of Villa-Lobos. Brazil widened its horizons and incorporated creative aspects of other regions of the country in the Rio–São Paulo axis. In this atmosphere, the manifold talents of Di Cavalcanti, thinker, "talker" and artist, flourished.

Di Cavalcanti (1897–1976), who was born in Rio de Janeiro, even wrote a book that reflects his personality and his love for the city: *Reminiscências líricas de um perfeito carioca* (Lyrical Reminiscences of a Perfect Carioca). He loved the daily life of the city and sought to represent the passion he felt for the rhythmic movements of samba, the colourful magic of Carnaval and the "dangerous" curves of women of mixed descent, a recurring theme in his painting.

STATUE OF JOÃO CAETANO

Teatro João Caetano
Praça Tiradentes
Centro
• Metro: Carioca

A shifting statue

The statue of actor João Caetano dos Santos, opposite the João Caetano Theatre, originally stood in front of the nearby Academia Imperial de Belas Artes (Imperial Academy of Fine Arts). The statue was moved in 1916, during renovation work carried out by the Banco do Brasil. The actor is dressed as Oscar, Son of Ossian, one of his best-known roles.

For more about the theatre, see next page.

REMAINS OF THE ACADEMIA IMPERIAL DE BELAS ARTES

Opened in 1826, the Imperial Academy of Fine Arts was considered to be the most beautiful building in Rio. Designed by the "father" of architectural teaching in Brazil, Grandjean de Montigny, it was demolished in 1938. Nothing has yet been built in its place, incredible as that may sound ...

Besides the João Caetano statue, the Academy's entrance gate was preserved and is now at the Botanical Garden (see p. 120).

The last vestige, which is more subtle, is the semicircular plaza at the corner of Travessa das Belas Artes and Rua Imperatriz Leopoldina. Although Montigny had wanted to build the plaza since 1836 to provide a better view of the Academy, especially its magnificent gateway, it wasn't finished until 1847. Rua Imperatriz Leopoldina was opened three years later, in 1850, the first "circular square" in Brazil.

THE CURSE OF TEATRO JOÃO CAETANO

In 1813, the João Caetano Theatre was partly built with stones originally intended for the cathedral in Largo de São Francisco de Paula (now the Institute of Philosophy and Social Sciences, nearby). As the latter work was interrupted, the stones were reused for the theatre's foundations. Some saw this as sacrilegious and the origins of the curse on the theatre, which suffered three fires in less than thirty years: in 1824, 1831 and 1839. Demolished and rebuilt in Art Deco style in 1928 (see photo), the theatre was again completely restored in 1978 to become what it is today.

For some, the present building is an architectural carbuncle in the heart of the city and the curse that hovers over it is omnipresent – how else to explain the fact that after being built in four different but equally attractive styles (three classical and one Art Deco), its current configuration is so unharmonious? Wouldn't the solution be to demolish it once and for all to open up the view between Praça Tiradentes and the Real Gabinete Real da Leitura (a library with a vast collection of volumes by Portuguese authors)?

RENT-A-SLAVE FOR AN EVENING AT THE THEATRE ...

In the colonial era, the theatre was a longstanding status symbol – it was a good thing to be seen there with slaves to show your importance. People who had no slaves could even hire them for the evening to give the impression of wealth.

GOLDEN ROSE OF THE MUSEU ARQUIDIOCESANO DE ARTE SACRA ⓭

Museu Arquidiocesano de Arte Sacra
Catedral Metropolitana de São Sebastião
245 Avenida República do Chile
• Open Wednesday 9am–12 noon and 1pm–4pm, Saturday and Sunday 9am–12 noon
• Other days, visits on reservation only, call (21) 2240-2669 / 2240-2869 / 2262-1797 (free access to cathedral 8am–5pm daily) • Admission to museum: R$2
• Metro: Carioca
• www.catedral.com.br

The princess's Golden Rose

The well-hidden (and seldom visited) Archdiocesan Museum of Sacred Art in the cathedral basement has a collection of over 5,000 pieces of religious art. Among them is a very special work.

At the back of the museum, on the left, curious visitors will find a Golden Rose presented by Pope Leo XIII (1810–1903) to Princess Isabel (1846–1921), daughter of Emperor Pedro II and acting regent of the Empire of Brazil. The rose, or rather bunch of roses, consists of a 45 cm stem with 12 branches, 24 thorns, 12 buds and 124 leaves. It rests in a neoclassical silver vase.

On 29 May 1888, a few days after the princess had signed the Lei Áurea (Golden Law) of 13 May that abolished slavery (Brazil was the last independent American country to free its slaves), Leo XIII signed the letter granting the Golden Rose. As he said to Isabel: "Do not look at the price of the object and its value, but be attentive to the most sacred mysteries it represents." He also stressed that the flower symbolises the majesty of Christ, and its fragrance "remotely permeates all those who scrupulously emulate its virtues".

The Golden Rose of Princess Isabel was kept by the Brazilian imperial family and donated to the Metropolitan Cathedral to mark the centenary of the birth of the princess.

WHAT IS THE GOLDEN ROSE?

The Golden Rose is a sacred ornament that usually depicts a single rose (sometimes a spray of roses) in solid gold. Every year, the pope would present one to a sovereign, a place of worship or pilgrimage, or even an entire community, as a special mark of honour.

Since many of these precious objects were subsequently melted down for their gold, only a few rare examples still exist: one in the Treasury of the Basilica of St Marks in Venice, one in the Musée de Cluny in Paris, one in the Palazzo Comunale of Siena (Tuscany), two in the Treasury of the Hofburg in Vienna, one in the Treasury of the Cathedral of Benevento (southern Italy) and one in the Museum of Sacred Art in the Vatican Library. More recent popes (including John Paul II) have presented Golden Roses to Lourdes, to the Brazilian basilica of Nossa Senhora Aparecida (1967 and 2007) and to the Sanctuary of Guadalupe (Mexico).

Although the first mention of such a Golden Rose was in 1049, in a papal bull issued by Pope Leo IX, the earliest mention of one being presented by a pope dates from the end of the 11th century: in 1098–1099, Urban II gave one to Count Foulques d'Anjou for preaching the First Crusade.

As the message that always accompanies it makes clear, the Golden Rose is a secular honour with spiritual significance. Just as the rose is considered the most beautiful and highly perfumed of all flowers, its presentation as a gift expresses the pontiff's wish that the heart and spirit of the recipient will be bathed in an equally divine fragrance.

THE SLAB OF CONCRETE FROM GALEÃO RUNWAY THAT POPE JOHN PAUL II KISSED

There are two other eye-catching pieces in the museum collection. When John Paul II came to Rio for the first time, he kissed the ground as usual on alighting at Galeão International Airport on 1 July 1980. This piece of the runway is now in the museum.

In a showcase near this exhibit is the "Pope's ring". When the pope went through the *favela* of Vidigal during the same papal visit, he took the gold ring off his finger and donated it to the community. Since 1982, it has been part of the museum collection. The Archdiocese has had a silver replica made, which was displayed in the chapel of São Francisco de Assis (St Francis of Assisi), built by Vidigal residents as a joint project for the pope's visit. The replica ring was stolen years later and a new one made. For security reasons, a small group of residents now take it in turns to keep the ring. As a result of this theft, the chapel that had become known as the "Pope's Chapel" was sealed off. Nowadays, however, it opens once a fortnight for Mass.

AZULEJOS AT THE CLUBE DOS DEMOCRÁTICOS ⑳

93 Rua do Riachuelo
Lapa

> ### *Three delightful and little-known panels*

The upper façade of the Democrats Club headquarters – built in 1930 by Sebastião Oliveira, and one of the major Carnaval schools of the early decades of the 20th century – features three delightful and little-known *azulejo* panels. Themes include Pierrot and Columbine and two chorus girls talking to Charlie Chaplin. The design is attributed to cartoonist Trinas Fox.

In the lobby, pretty female figures in polychrome stucco relief show dancers clad in brief costumes, highlighting the carnival theme.

The front entrance, with its geometric lines and refined aesthetics, also demonstrates the marriage between carnival caricatures and the streamlined architecture typical of a modern metropolis.

ESCOLA DE MÚSICA CONCERT HALL ㉑

98 Rua do Passeio
Lapa
• Metro: Cinelândia
• Occasionally open to the public, free concerts
• www.musica.ufrj.br

> **A forgotten gem**

Although the Rio Music School building (next to the Automobile Club) is well known to Cariocas, few have crossed its threshold. Which is a pity, because its lovely façade leads to one of the city's finest interiors, with a delightfully old-fashioned atmosphere.

To see inside, take a look at the programme of free concerts regularly held there.

One of the monumental staircases will take you first of all to the charming foyer facing the entrance to the concert hall. This room is worth a visit: its terrace has a delightful and unusual view of downtown Rio. The main attraction, however, is the group of four beautiful frescoes on the theme of music, executed in 1922 by Brazilian artist and designer Antônio Parreiras. The Art Nouveau style of "*Osiris – Inventor of the Flute*" and "*Seven Notes*" is particularly successful.

The concert hall itself, inspired by the Salle Gaveau (former headquarters of the famous piano makers in Paris), is one of the largest in the country and known for its excellent acoustics.

With the proclamation of the Republic in 1889, the former conservatory, dating from 1848, became a national music institute. The first director was composer Leopoldo Miguez (1850–1902), who gave his name to the concert hall. On his appointment, he travelled to Europe to visit various conservatories and observe different teaching methods. The institute moved in 1913 and the present building dates from 1922.

INVERNO STATUE IN THE PASSEIO PÚBLICO **㉒**

Entrance via Rua do Passeio, between Lapa and Cinelândia
• Open daily
• Free
• Metro: Cinelândia

> **A statue disappears then reappears, sanctified**

The *Inverno* (Winter) statue in the Passeio Público, originally unveiled in 1861 along with three other works (together representing the four seasons), disappeared for a good part of the 20th century.

The statue was eventually found in 2000 in the gardens of the Centro Cultural Municipal Laurinda Santos Lobo, Santa Tereza, and replaced in the public park the same year. It's said that when the statue of the "saint" was removed from the cultural centre, local devotees made the curious request that she should remain there as they now worshipped *Nossa Senhora de Ferro* (Our Iron Lady), as they called her.

A FOUL SMELL THAT LED TO THE PARK BEING RENOVATED

The Passeio Público, the public park built in the 18th century in the style of a French formal garden by Mestre Valentim da Fonseca e Silva (1745–1813), underwent a major renovation after the embarrassing experience of Prince Maximilian of Austria in January 1860. Strolling along the terrace, with its pavilions offering magnificent views over Guanabara bay, he couldn't stand the overpowering stench and held his nose with a handkerchief. So Dom Pedro II decided to renovate the park and French botanist and landscaper Auguste Glaziou (1833–1906) – called the "landscaper of the empire" for his many projects in Rio – was commissioned for the job. With Glaziou, the gardens reverted to the English style. He cut down a number of trees and replanted other large species that are still there today, and installed the four seasons statues, cast at Val d'Osne in France.

SEA VIEW

The Passeio Público was built on land reclaimed from the lagoon of Boqueirão da Ajuda, considered a "pestilential swamp". Lying beside Guanabara bay, its banks were very busy. With the opening of Avenida Beira-Mar in 1906, however, the site was further from the shore, and even further away after Aterro do Flamengo was reclaimed from the sea in 1965.

REMAINS OF A FOUNTAIN RECALLING THE VICEROY'S FORBIDDEN LOVE

At the far end of the park is all that remains of the Fonte dos Amores (Love Fountain). This fountain, designed by Mestre Valentim, was thought to have been inspired by the passion of Viceroy Luís de Vasconcelos (1742–1809) for Suzana, a poor girl who lived in a shack at the edge of the lagoon. Elements of the fountain, also known as Fonte dos Jacarés (Crocodile Fountain), symbolise the characters in this romance. Two centuries later, it was the inspiration for the Portela samba school, who sang about the "Carioca Legend: Dreams of the Viceroy" at the 1988 Carnaval.

The Crocodile Fountain, the two granite pyramids facing it and the entrance gate are the criteria under which the Passeio Público is classified as national heritage.

THE FIRST PUBLIC PARK IN THE AMERICAS

Inaugurated in 1783, almost a hundred years before New York's Central Park, the Passeio Público was the first public park in the Americas.

SECRETS OF THE INSTITUTO HISTÓRICO E GEOGRÁFICO BRASILEIRO

㉓

8 Avenida Augusto Severo, Glória
• Open: Mon-Fri 1pm—5pm
• Free entry
• Reservations by phone: (21) 2252-4430 / 2509-5107
• www.ihgb.org.br
• Metro: Cinelândia

> *The oldest waymarker in Brazil, a foundlings' wheel and a spectacular view ...*

Book a visit to the Brazilian Historical and Geographical Institute (IHGB), housed in a central building in the Glória neighbourhood, to appreciate some of its interesting and little-known aspects.

The salão nobre (great hall) holds a historical treasure: the Marco de Cananéia - the oldest waymarker in Brazil. This type of stone marker, carved with a flared cross (cross pattée, like that of the Knights Templar) and the shield of Portugal, was used to designate regions where Jesuits had settled. The stones were originally used as ballast by the caravels that sailed from Portugal to Brazil laden with precious timber. This one is thought to have been set up on Ilha do Cardoso (near Cananéia and the other islands of a small archipelago on the south coast of São Paulo) by the expedition commanded by Gaspar de Lemos that landed there on 24 January 1502. The navigator and cartographer was the Italian Amerigo Vespucci, who was honoured by having the newly discovered continent named after him. The stone was found at Ponta do Itacuruçá and transported to the IHGB in the mid-19th century. A replica is kept on Cardoso.

On the 12th floor of the museum is a foundlings' wheel that was originally installed at Rua Evaristo da Veiga, next to the military police barracks. Any children abandoned there were handed over to the Santa Casa da Misericórdia in Rua Santa Luzia (for more on foundlings' wheels see p. 167).

Finally, the terrace on the 13th floor offers a spectacular view of the eclectic architecture of the city centre.

Cananéia is considered to be the oldest settlement in Brazil. Marataiama (its original name) was founded by Portuguese explorer and colonial administrator Martim Afonso de Souza in 1531. As there is no documentary evidence to prove this, some claim that the country's first city was São Vicente, whose archives confirm that it was founded on 22 January 1532, also by Afonso de Souza.

The institute's great hall, nowadays only used for plenary and special sessions, houses the preserved rosewood chair on which Dom Pedro II sat during the 506 IHGB sessions he presided over.

UNFINISHED PAINTING OF PEDRO II'S CORONATION

The great hall also features a very special painting. On the back wall hangs an unfinished canvas entitled *Coroação de Pedro II* (Coronation of Pedro II) by Manuel de Araújo Porto Alegre (1806–1879). He began the painting just after the coronation in July 1841, but as the government failed to confirm that it would buy the work, he never finished it. Curiously enough, the following year, Pedro II decorated the French painter François-René Moreaux (1807–1860) to reward him for his painting also depicting the coronation (now displayed in the Museu Imperial de Petrópolis). The unfinished canvas was stored in the cellar of the Escola Nacional de Belas Artes (National School of Fine Arts, now National Museum of Fine Arts) for almost a century before coming to the IHGB.

Central do Brasil

Central ⓜ

Presidente Vargas ⓜ

PRAÇA DA REPÚBLICA

Campo de Santana

Avenida Presidente Vargas

Rua de Santana

Rua Frei Caneca

PRAÇA TIRADENTES

Carioca ⓜ

CENTRO

Catedral de São Sebastião

Cinelândia

PRAÇA DA CRUZ VERMELHA

Rua Salvador de Sá

Viaduto São Pedro

Túnel Martim de Sá

Av. Mem de Sá

Rua Frei Caneca

Cinelândia ⓜ Dantes

Av. Pres. Wilson

Parque Passeio Público

Museu de Arte Moderna

BAIRRO DE FÁTIMA

CATUMBI

Rua Itapiru

Rua Almirante Alexandrino

Ensea da Gló

GLÓRIA

PRAÇA PARIS

20-21
22

L. DA GLÓRIA

Glória ⓜ

❶
❷
❸
❹

23

Morro da Coroa
127 m

R. Monte Alegre

Rua Santo Amaro

Morro Santo Amaro
68 m

Museu da República

SANTA TERESA

Rua Itapiru

Rua Bento Lisboa

Rua Silveira Martins

Catete

Av. Beira Mar

Av. Infante Dom Henrique

Praia do Flamengo

Morro Nova Cintra
261 m

Túnel Santa Bárbara

Rua do Catete

19

Alexandrino

Rua Almirante

Túnel do Comprido Laranjeiras

Rua Pereira da Silva

Parque E. Guinle

Largo do Machado ⓜ

Rua das Laranjeiras

PRAÇA JOSÉ ALENCAR

16

LARANJEIRAS

Rua Alice

FLAMENGO

❺

17 **18**

Rua das Laranjeiras

R. Cardoso Junior

9

Rua Pinheiro Machado

Paissandu

Rua Flamengo

8

Morro Azul
66 m

Rua Marquês de Abrantes

❻

PRAÇA CUAUHTEMOQUE

Rua Senador Vergueiro

Rua Cosme Velho

15

Rua General Glicério

10

Morro Mundo Novo
130 m

Rua Barão de Itambi

PRAÇA MARINHA DO BRASIL

Av. Osvaldo Cruz

Morro da Viúva
77 m

❼

Túnel André Rebouças

Rua

Morro Dona Marta
364 m

R. Marquês Olinda

Rua Bambina

Av. das Nações Unidas

Praia de Botafogo

Enseada de Botafogo

São Clemente

Botafogo ⓜ

PRAÇA PIMENTEL DUARTE

Morro do Pasmado
63 m

14

PRAÇA CORUMBÁ

Rua

BOTAFOGO

Parque Y. Rabin

PRAÇA ENG. BERNARDO SATAO

Av. Pasteur

Rua Humaitá

Rua Conde de Irajá

Rua Voluntários da Pátria

Rua Real Grandeza

Rua Paulo Barreto

Rua Sorocaba

R. Prof. Alvaro Rodrigues

Rua Arnaldo Quintela

Rua Alvaro Ramos

Av. Venceslau Braz

Av. Lauro Sodré

R. Lauro Muller

HUMAITÁ

Rua Humaitá

Rua Visconde de Silva

Rua General Polidoro

13

11

Cemitério de São João Batista

12

Mo da Babilo
238

0   500   1 000

N

BOTAFOGO - FLAMENGO LARANJEIRAS - CATETE GLORIA - STA TERESA

BAS-RELIEF STATUE OF SÃO SEBASTIÃO ❶

Praça Luís de Camões (also known as Largo do Russel)
Glória
• Metro: Glória

The miraculous appearance of St Sebastian

Although Cariocas are well aware of the statue of São Sebastião (St Sebastian) in Largo do Russel, few realise its significance.

It was here, in July 1566, that the Portuguese soldiers led by Estácio de Sá claimed that St Sebastian had appeared. Thanks to this divine intervention, the Portuguese defeated the French at the famous battle "das Canoas" (of the canoes). The following year, on 20 January (the saint's feast day), victory at the battle of Uruçu-mirim (near where Morro da Glória church now stands) consolidated the Portuguese presence and resulted in the expulsion of the French from the island colony known as France Antarctique. Estácio de Sá was seriously wounded by an arrow, just like St Sebastian, patron of the city, and died a month later from his injuries.

The battle of the canoes and belief in the intervention of St Sebastian are immortalised on the base of the statue, a bas-relief depicting a battle scene, with the title "Apparition of St Sebastian at the Battle against the Canoes". Just below is an inscription that translates as: "Just to be called city of St Sebastian is to be favoured by the Lord and by the merits of the Glorious Martyr."

The 7 m statue by sculptor Dante Crossi was erected in 1965, in commemoration of the fourth centenary of the founding of the city.

The representation of the saint hanging from a tree trunk, wounded by three arrows, is inspired by a statue of St Sebastian brought to Rio de Janeiro in the 16th century.

Portuguese sailors were the first to discover Guanabara bay on 1 January 1502. Believing the entrance to the bay to be the mouth of a river, they named it Rio de Janeiro. It was only in March 1565 that the city was founded, upon the arrival of Estácio de Sá to attack the French. It was given the name "São Sebastião do Rio de Janeiro" in homage to the then king of Portugal, Dom Sebastião.

At the time that the city was founded, Glória hill sometimes resembled an island as there were so many sources of water in the region. Just opposite was a beach, later named Praia do Russel (before it was built over), as well as a swamp (which became Largo da Glória after landfill) and the Catete river, now also in a culvert (see p. 58).

GETÚLIO VARGAS MEMORIAL ❷

Praça Luís de Camões (also known as Largo do Russel)
Glória
• Open Tuesday to Sunday 10am–5pm
• Admission free
• Metro: Glória

A poignant but little-known site

Despite the high profile of the bust of Getúlio Vargas, 2.5 m high and installed on a base of 3 m on Largo do Russel, it's strange that his memorial is so little known by Cariocas – perhaps because it stands in a basement that can't be seen from the street and is only accessible down a discreet flight of steps. In a large quiet space, with soft lighting, the memorial has a permanent exhibition of photographs, texts (in Portuguese and English), videos and objects relating to the life of the former president and some aspects of the history of Brazil and Rio de Janeiro.

During his forty-five years of public life, Getúlio Vargas lived for nearly three decades in the city that was then the country's capital. After the 1930 revolution, of which he was the main leader, Vargas was head of the interim government, President of the Republic elected by the National Congress, dictator and finally President of the Republic elected by the people.

The exhibition is divided into eight sections. Apart from showing the political and social context and the actions of the government of the day, they highlight Cariocas' relationship with the head of state and the impact of government policy on the city. You can, for example, see little-known photographs of urban reform undertaken during the Estado Novo (1937–1945, the period of the Vargas dictatorship); snapshots of the construction of Avenida Presidente Vargas, for which 525 buildings and 4 churches were demolished; the opening of Avenida Brasil; the construction of Santos Dumont

Airport; and the urbanisation of Esplanada do Castelo, where the Ministries of Finance, Labour, Education and Health (see p. 51) were built.

The final sections of the exhibition are devoted to the intense political and military pressure that led Vargas to commit suicide with a bullet through the heart on 24 August 1954, at the nearby Catete Palace (153 Rua do Catete). The photos on display at the memorial as the last tribute to the president, in particular one of the crowd accompanying the funeral procession to Santos Dumont airport, are impressive and moving.

> The memorial monument stands 17.5 m high – no higher than the treetops so as not to obstruct the neighbouring buildings' view of the sea.

MEMORIAL COMMEMORATING THE OPENING OF THE PORTS IN 1808 ❸

Avenida Beira Mar
• Metro: Glória

The other vestige commemorating the opening of the ports in 1808

Although the centenary of the opening of the ports to friendly nations (see opposite) was celebrated with great pomp with a National Exposition at Urca (see p. 200), it was also commemorated in 1908 right here beside the former Hotel Glória by two flights of ornamental steps, a balustrade and two statues.

The statues, by French sculptor Eugène Bénet, were inspired by those of Place de la Concorde in Paris. They represent trade (a seated woman holding a caduceus, the symbol of commerce, on the Flamengo side) and navigation (a seated woman holding an anchor in her left hand, on the Largo do Russel side). At the foot of each statue, facing Rua do Russel, an inscription is engraved in the stone: 28 January 1808 – opening of the ports.

The date 1908 (in Roman numerals: MCMVIII) can be seen at the foot of each statue, facing Avenida Beira Mar, with a small plaque explaining the historical context.

OPENING OF THE PORTS IN 1808: A BRITISH CONDITION IN EXCHANGE FOR HELPING JOÃO VI OF PORTUGAL TO FLEE TO BRAZIL

In 1806, Napoleon had Portugal against the wall. The Portuguese prince regent (the future King João VI) was summoned to join the blockade against Great Britain, otherwise the French would invade his country. The Portuguese sovereign was faced with a dilemma: the alliance with France and joining the blockade would mean Portugal breaking with Great Britain, the end of trade with its colonies and the loss of his empire, which he could not resign himself to. This is what revived the long-standing project to transfer the Portuguese court to Brazil, proposed in 1803 by his adviser Dom Rodrigo de Sousa Coutinho.

October 1807: precipitating events, Napoleon ordered the immediate invasion of Portugal. On 18 October, General Junot crossed the French–Spanish border at the head of an army of 25,000 men on their way to Portugal. The advance went less smoothly than expected.

On 29 November, at the last moment, a Portuguese fleet of sixteen ships containing 15,000 people (the royal family, courtesans, aristocrats, the bourgeoisie, civil servants, senior officials and a considerable number of Portuguese officers) left Portugal for Brazil. The prince regent and his entourage took with them the crown art collections, the state archives, the royal treasury, and even the silverware from churches and the Royal Library.

At 9am the next day, Junot arrived in the deserted Portuguese capital with his 25,000 men.

The flight of the King of Portugal was facilitated by the British, on one condition: he was to decree the opening of Brazilian ports to trade as soon as possible. Until then, Brazil had only been allowed to trade with Portugal, which had a monopoly of trade with the colony (colonial pact): incredible as it may seem today, nothing could be bought or sold in Brazil without physically passing through Portugal.

On 28 January 1808, four days after his arrival in Salvador on his way to Rio, João VI signed the decree authorising the opening of the ports. This allowed goods to be traded directly with Brazil, bypassing Portugal, which was in Napoleon's hands.

Although João VI obviously had no choice, the major beneficiaries of this agreement were the British, who negotiated particularly favourable customs tariffs.

At the time, the ocean reached the foot of the steps and Avenida Beira Mar, which was opened in 1906. Not until 1922, when Morro do Castelo was levelled (see p. 61), were the beaches of Santa Luzia (Castelo), Ajuda (Cinelândia), Glória, Russel and Boqueirão (opposite the Passeio Público, see p. 120) as far as Calabouço (near the National Historical Museum) built over. For more on the amount of land reclaimed by the city of Rio, see p. 58.

VILLINO SILVEIRA DOORWAY ❹

734 Rua do Russel
Glória
• Metro: Glória

Golden serpents doorway

Villino Silveira (1915), designed by the Italian architect Antonio Virzi, is one of the city's most unusual houses. It was intended to be the residence of the Elixir de Nogueira manufacturer and Carioca entrepreneur, Gervásio Renault da Silveira.

This large villa, wedged between two other buildings and quite unlike its surroundings, is perhaps Rio's best example of Art Nouveau. It features a wrought-iron gate with a cleverly executed design by the Italian manufacturer Pagani. The handles are gilded serpents amid a profusion of rays blending sinuous and angular shapes. The hinges at the top corners, often unnoticed, are covered by what appears to be a prehistoric bird's beak in miniature.

The house, which was listed as a historic monument in 1970, was acquired in the 1990s by the nearby Hotel Glória and converted into a café, now closed.

"IF HE'D DONE THE SAME IN ITALY, HE'D HAVE BEEN AN INTERNATIONALLY RENOWNED ARCHITECT"

Virzi's architecture, like that of Antoni Gaudí, is unpredictable: from asymmetrical columns to fine stucco details, through window guardrails delicately worked in steel.

Arriving in Rio in 1910, Virzi was a professor at the National School of Fine Arts and designed properties for the most extravagant Carioca bourgeoisie. "If he'd done the same in Italy, he'd have been an internationally renowned architect," according to architect Alberto Taveira at the National Institute for Cultural Heritage. Unfortunately, few of his achievements survive today. Apart from this house, there are only four of his buildings in the city: Casa Villino Silveira (see opposite), the amazing Casa Villiot at Copacabana (see p. 175), Nossa Senhora de Lourdes basilica at Vila Isabel, and a warehouse at Catumbi.

The architect's other spectacular buildings have been demolished, including the Elixir de Nogueira plant (62 Rua da Glória) in 1970 and the Smith de Vasconcelos villa (680 Avenida Atlântica) in 1964.

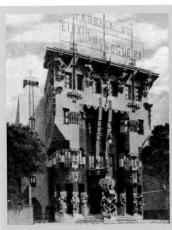

The "miraculous" Elixir de Nogueira, the recipe for which includes walnuts, parsley, jacaranda and guaiac, dates from a time when it was believed that many diseases were caused by impurities in the blood. The elixir was advertised as a "great blood purifier". Product labels were artistically designed and generally bore an image of its inventor, pharmacist João da Silva Silveira from Pelotas.

MONUMENT TO THE CARIOCA RIVER ❺

Praça José de Alencar
Flamengo
• Metro: Flamengo or Largo do Machado

> *Tribute
> to the unseen
> river*

The first thing you'll notice on reaching Praça José de Alencar is the monument to the Brazilian novelist who gave his name to the plaza – it has stood there since 1897. To his left, with your back to the Parque do Flamengo, you'll also see a strange lamp, with a curved post attached to a concrete base. On the ground are three metallic circles of different sizes. Inside are concentric circles with two circular openings at the centre that look like spectacles, dotted with small lozenges.

If the first thing this brings to mind is upmarket manhole covers, the circles on the ground are actually the remains of little fountains (no longer working), a reminder to Cariocas that the Carioca river (see p. 136-137) is flowing under their feet towards its mouth at Praia do Flamengo. This project by architect Mario Jorge Jauregui is a tribute to the forgotten river that has played such an important role in the city's history.

The redevelopment of the plaza, which saw the installation of lighting and the circles on the ground, dates from 1990 and was part of the various Rio-Cidade urban planning schemes in many of the city's neighbourhoods. The

controversial inclined poles at Ipanema are a well-known example from this time. Lack of maintenance, and in some cases vandalism, have undermined the original aims, as in the case of the fountains in Praça José de Alencar.

The statue of José de Alencar, the work of Mexican sculptor Rodolfo Bernardelli (1852–1931), a naturalised Brazilian, was unveiled in 1897. On its base are carved bas-relief scenes from four of the writer's great novels: *Iracema*, *O Guarani*, *O Gaúcho* and *O Sertanejo*. Nationalism, which highlights a typically Brazilian way of feeling and thinking, is a prominent feature of his work. José de Alencar (1829–1877) was also a journalist, lawyer and politician.

FORMER COURSE OF THE CARIOCA RIVER

The source of the Carioca is in the Serra da Carioca, Tijuca forest. The river flows below Cosme Velho, Laranjeiras and Flamengo streets before it reaches the bay. Except at its source and mouth, the river can only be seen from the beautiful although poorly maintained Largo do Boticário, the small courtyard near Corcovado tram station in Cosme Velho. Its course was blocked off in the early 20th century.

At one time, the Carioca divided into two at what is now Praça José Alencar (see opposite), where there was a lake. This is where the Salema bridge stood, the city's first, built by Governor António Salema between 1574 and 1577. From there, some of the water flowed towards the mouth of the river, as far as Praia do Flamengo, and the rest was diverted to the left. The branch of the river leading to Flamengo beach has survived, although it flows underground. The water is so polluted that it is treated at a plant in Flamengo park before it reaches the beach.

The other branch of the river, known as the Catete, runs through a culvert under what is now Rua do Catete. It skirts the Morro da Glória to reach the sea at the former Russel beach – now built over to form a plaza with a statue of São Sebastião (St Sebastian, see p. 127) and the Memorial Municipal Getúlio Vargas (see p. 128).

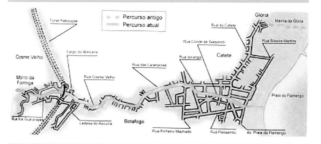

ORIGIN OF THE WORD *CARIOCA*

Although there is no consensus about the origin of the word *carioca*, it is probably of Tupi Indian origin and refers to a stone house built in the early 16th century at Flamengo, near the mouth of the river.

The Indians called it *akari oca*, i.e. the house of *acari*. Perhaps as an early manifestation of Carioca humour, there are at least two amusing explanations for the etymology of this name: it was the first time that Indians had seen men living in a stone dwelling, like the *acari* fish, so they called the building "the house of *acari*". The other explanation is that *acari* also means "catfish", the nickname given to the Portuguese because of their armour. *Akari oca* evolved into *carioca*, which became the name of the river and, over time, the word used for those born in the city.

RIVER, AQUEDUCT, SPRING, FOUNTAIN, PLAZA, STREET: THE IMPORTANCE TO RIO OF THE CARIOCA

The Carioca river was so important (it was used as a source of drinking water for centuries) that the name was bestowed on the places and buildings directly connected with it. The source was known as the Serra da Carioca. The Aqueduto da Carioca (Carioca Aqueduct, generally known as the Arcos da Lapa or Lapa Arches) carried the waters of the river, diverted to Santo Antônio *morro* from Santa Teresa, to reach what later became the Chafariz da Carioca (Carioca Fountain), in Campo da Santo Antônio – the current Largo da Carioca, which is connected to Praça Tiradentes by Rua da Carioca.

The marble fountain, which has sixteen bronze spouts, was the country's first public fountain. Inaugurated in 1723 (the same year as the aqueduct), it was demolished in 1820. The waters of the Carioca were so popular that they inspired the phrase "This is as good as Carioca water". For obvious reasons, this saying is now obsolete …

PEDRA EXTRAHIDA
DA
GRUTA DE LOURDES

GRUTA DE LOURDES, IGREJA DA SANTISSIMA ⑥ TRINDADE

141 Rua Senador Vergueiro
• Open Monday to Friday 7am–12 noon and 2pm–6pm; Sunday 7.30am–12 noon and 4pm–8pm
• Tel: (21) 2553-3114
• E-mail: sstrindade.rj@gmail.com
• www.sstrindade.com

> *A reproduction of the grotto of Our Lady of Lourdes*

Cariocas often forget about the Church of the Holy Trinity at Flamengo, yet it has two unusual features: a lovely Art Deco façade designed by French architect Henri Sajous, who worked in Brazil between 1930 and 1959; and, less conspicuous, a reproduction of the famous grotto of Our Lady of Lourdes (in France), in the courtyard behind the church.

The grotto was the brainchild of Father Aleixo Chauvin, who arrived in Rio in 1937 with a stone from Massabielle at Lourdes, where the Virgin Mary had appeared eighteen times to Bernadette Soubirous. Father Chauvin was hoping to build a replica of the famous grotto in Brazil. Funded by a Brazilian family living in France, the Rio grotto opened in May 1939, before the present church was built. Construction began in 1940 following the arrival in Rio of the Augustinians of the Assumption in 1935, following the invitation of Cardinal Sebastião Leme, and was completed in 1945.

The congregation of Catholic brothers, also known as Assumptionists, was founded in Nimes by Father Emmanuel d'Alzon in 1845. The *Rule of Life* adopted by the congregation draws its inspiration from that of St Augustine of Hippo. The brothers were especially devoted to the Assumption of the Virgin Mary, which explains her role in the pilgrimage to Lourdes on 15 August (Feast of the Assumption).

As part of their mission, the Assumptionists have established replicas of the Lourdes grotto throughout the world – apart from Rio, they are found in Tokyo, Montreal, New York, Dublin and Milan (see *Secret Tokyo*, *Secret Montreal*, *Secret New York*, *Secret Dublin* and *Secret Milan* in this series of guides).

Each motif on the church's 21 stained-glass windows corresponds to one of the 137 windows of Chartres Cathedral in France.

MORRO DA VIÚVA

❼

Access by Travessa Acaraí
• Metro: Botafogo

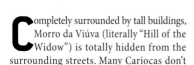

One of the city's great secrets

Completely surrounded by tall buildings, Morro da Viúva (literally "Hill of the Widow") is totally hidden from the surrounding streets. Many Cariocas don't even know it exists.

And yet, while some blocks have built-in access to the hill itself (with sports and other facilities for the happy few living in the surrounding buildings), there is an official secret way for the public to get onto the *morro*: at the end of Avenida Oswaldo Cruz, on the Botafogo side, the dead-end street called Travessa Acaraí leads to a small door that you just push to open.

Don't hesitate: a Rio police chief lives at the corner and the place is considered to be very safe.

The idea of accessing one of the city's truly hidden corners is especially exciting for people who are not afraid of urban exploration and enjoy climbing the 195 steps that lead to the ruins of a former reservoir.

Built by Antônio Gabrielli in 1891 to supply drinking water to the Botafogo, Praia Vermelha and Leme districts, the reservoir was closed in 1970 and partially listed in 1998. Now abandoned, it's part of an area where six families leading very frugal lives will usually be happy to help you discover places with a view through the trees to Botafogo beach, Pedra da Gávea and Corcovado on on one side, and Sugarloaf Mountain on the other.

WHERE DOES THE NAME MORRO DA VIÚVA COME FROM?

Morro da Viúva (Hill of the Widow) was so named in 1753, when it became the property of Dona Joaquina Figueiredo Pereira Barros, on the death of her husband Joaquim José Gomes de Barros. The hill was previously named Morro do Léry, or Morro do Leryfe, after the French Protestant missionary Jean de Léry, who came to Brazil with the Huguenots under Villegaignon in the 16th century and lived in a stone house nearby.

Avenida Rui Barbosa, which skirts the *morro* on the shore side, was built in 1922.

Before the reservoir was there, fortifications had been built on this site in 1863 at a time when tensions between Brazil and Britain were high (the "Christie question", from the name of the British ambassador at the time, William Dougal Christie). The strategic and military importance of the place was soon questioned, however, and the fort was little used.

CASA MARAJOARA

8

319 Rua Paissandu
• Metro: Flamengo
• Private residence

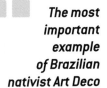

> **The most important example of Brazilian nativist Art Deco**

Casa Marajoara (Marajoara House) at 319 Rua Paissandu is the most important example of the nativist trend in Brazilian Art Deco architecture, with its direct references to indigenous influences on everyday life that are still felt today.

The architectural mass of the house, a project of Gilson Gladstone Navarro dating from 1937, suggests the influence of Californian bungalows and North American "pueblo" architecture, but has indisputable traces of Brazilian indigenous themes. Its nativism goes so far as to take in the name of the street (see opposite).

The cladding, which is almost entirely of polished ashlar, demonstrates the extent to which Carioca climatic variations have been taken into account. In summer, a cool internal temperature is guaranteed thanks to the thick stone covering the façade. During the mild tropical winters, the same stone cladding provides residents with a sense of well-being.

There are numerous references to Amazonian talismans (see p. 187): on all the gates and iron railings, as on the interior windows, a discreet frog-

shaped *muiraquitã* (ancient amulet) appears as a kind of leitmotiv. At the entrance, a stylised stone dragon, equally discreet, protects the place from evil.

The interior decoration of this private residence is unique in the nativist history of Brazilian Art Deco: wood panelling in sucupira (Brazilian chestnut) wood, with motifs from Marajoara art; hammered-metal lamp fixtures that repeat the same patterns; sliding doors on which life-size portraits of Indians are etched on the glass ...

Another two long-gone houses were inspired by indigenous peoples. The first was the house in Avenida Portugal, Urca, which belonged to Ernesto Simões Filho, Minister of Education under Getúlio Vargas. The second was the house designed by Edgard Pinheiro Vianna on Avenida Atlântica, known as the "house of stone". Both were demolished in the late 1980s.

The name "Paysandú" comes from a Uruguayan city that was the scene of the historic episode known as the "taking of Paysandú" (2 January 1865) in the Paraguayan War. It involved Brazilian troops and squadrons under General Mena Barreto (who has a street named after him near Rua Paissandu) and Admiral Tamandaré.

Rua Paissandu began at the palace where Princess Isabel and her husband, the Count of Eu (Gaston d'Orléans), lived in the 19th century. It continued as far as Praia do Flamengo, with imperial palm trees bordering the entire route.

STAINED-GLASS WINDOWS AT FLUMINENSE FOOTBALL CLUB ⑨

41 Rua Álvaro Chaves, Laranjeiras
• Open Tuesday to Sunday 10am—5pm
• R$15 for non-members, free for members
• Metro: Flamengo
• Tel: (21) 3179-7400
• www.fluminense.com.br

I f members of the Fluminense Club are familiar with the beauty of their surroundings, few others know that anyone can visit this very exclusive club.

Hidden beauty of an aristocratic club

The neoclassical club building, next to Guanabara Palace (see p. 148), is the work of architect Hipólito Pujol and was opened on 18 November 1920.

Its main salon has three beautiful stained-glass windows inspired by ancient Greece and the Roman Empire. Near the ceiling, the salon is decorated with stencils, delicate details with an intricate finish, which for years had been painted over. They were rediscovered during renovation work carried out between 2011 and 2014 and redone by hand, one by one. Also found during the restoration, beneath the ceiling paintwork, were canvases by the Timóteo da Costa brothers, who worked on the decoration of Copacabana Palace Hotel.

To the right of the club entrance, on the road leading to the tennis courts, don't miss a charming bas-relief of a tennis player in 1920s/30s style.

THE BALL FROM THE FIRST MATCH IN THE BRAZILIAN TEAM SELECTION

The club's trophy room (also open to the public) has an interactive exhibition showing important moments in the history of soccer in Brazil and Fluminense Stadium, which opened in 1919 with a match between Brazil and Chile. It is on this ground that the first match in the Brazilian team selection was played on 21 July 1914 (before the opening of the stadium). The ball from the match, which was attended by 5,000 spectators, is part of the collection.

The Brazilian amateurs then played against a professional team, Exeter City, from England. To everyone's surprise, Brazil won 2—0.

In 1984, the Rolling Stones recorded two video clips at the club – *Lucky in Love* and *Just Another Night*. For the first, the main salon was transformed into a casino, and for the second into a bar where you can spot an extra wearing the club's tricolour jersey. The band attended the final of the Carioca championship between Flamengo and Fluminense (Fluminense won 1—0).

PALÁCIO GUANABARA

Rua Pinheiro Machado, Laranjeiras
• Metro: Flamengo
• Free guided tours on Saturdays
• Tel: (21) 2334-3774 / 2334-3216 / 2334-3215
• Reservations at http://visitaguiada.casacivil.rj.gov.br/VisitaGuiada/

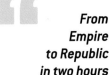

From Empire to Republic in two hours

Many Cariocas, let alone tourists, don't know that it's possible to visit Guanabara Palace, the state governor's office since 1960, when the capital was transferred to Brasilia.

This neoclassical edifice – built in 1853 by Portuguese trader José Machado Coelho as a private home – was acquired by the imperial government in 1865 for Princess Isabel, who had just married the French prince Gaston, Count of Eu. On the proclamation of the Republic in 1889, the palace passed into the hands of the Union: its ownership is still disputed between the descendants of the princess and the Brazilian state ...

The building has undergone several renovations over the years. The most recent, in 2011, revealed two beautiful examples of flooring from different eras. The first, on the ground floor, where the *senzala* (room reserved for slaves) would have been in Isabel's day, is made from stone in the *pé de moleque* style (see box). The well-preserved surface is covered with glass so that visitors can appreciate the original work. The other, at the entrance to the ground floor and repeated in the veranda on the first floor, is a mosaic of ceramic tiles. These works probably date from the great renovation of 1908, when the towers and façades were built, adding to the palace's eclectic air.

The canvas hanging in the main salon, *Morte de Estácio de Sá* by Brazilian painter and designer Antônio Parreiras, depicts some of the city founders: Estácio de Sá, Araribóia, Salvador de Sá and the Jesuit priests José de Anchieta and Manuel da Nóbrega. In the governor's office is a desk that belonged to President Getúlio Vargas and a painting by Brazilian artist Aurélio de Figueiredo, *Abdicação de D. Pedro I*, in which the seated child is the future Emperor Pedro II.

Behind the palace, the lovely landscaped garden, designed by French landscaper Paul Villon, stretches almost to the forest of Corcovado.

Since Princess Isabel lived there the palace has been put to several different uses – a barracks, to host illustrious guests, and the official residence of the President of the Republic between 1911 and 1949, when it became the seat of the federal legislature.

Pé de moleque is a technique for laying stone flooring dating from the colonial period. One hypothesis for the origin of this name is that the work was done by young people (*moleques*), who set the stones with their feet (*pe*). Others think it's because the floor resembles an almond dessert of the same name.

In the gardens to the left of the palace is the chapel of Santa Terezinha, built in 1946 at the request of Carmela Dutra, known as Dona Santinha, wife of President Eurico Gaspar Dutra. The altar, which is smaller than usual, was designed to allow Dona Santinha to see it from the window of her room in the palace.

In the 19th century, the main access to the palace was by Rua Paissandu, which was why it was planted with dozens of imperial palm trees. It's said that Princess Isabel liked to go from the palace to Flamengo beach, walking in the shade of the palms.

GRAVEYARD OF THE "LITTLE ANGELS" ⓫

Cemitério São João Batista
Rua General Polidoro / Rua Real Grandeza
• Open daily 9am—5pm
• Metro: Botafogo

> **One of the most secluded and moving places in the city**

The *anjinhos* (little angels) section of St John the Baptist cemetery is one of the most secluded, mysterious, strange and moving places in the entire city.

Take the main avenue after going through the main gateway on Rua General Polidoro. About halfway to the cemetery chapel (unfortunately closed) facing you, a path heads left towards the small bare hill in the north-east corner of the cemetery grounds, along Rua Álvaro Ramos.

At the foot of the hill, a flight of stone steps leads upwards, leaving behind the gentle murmur of the few visitors to the cemetery. The atmosphere changes very quickly: within seconds, you'll find yourself in a forested wilderness where the regular steps give way to an uneven stone path through the undergrowth. A few steps further and the mood changes again, ancient structures emerging here and there from the tropical vegetation in an atmosphere reminiscent of Colombia's "Lost City". After a few rather unsettling moments, you round the final bend at the top of the hill and are faced with an impressive array of white crosses stuck in the ground. Overcome by this vision (which of course inspires respect), you might think twice about walking through it, so retrace your steps and go left round the hill. On the other side, if you push back a branch that marks the end of the track, you emerge behind the same crosses, just as awesome. There is yet another field of crosses higher up on the left.

This uniquely moving and disturbing place is known as the "little angels" graveyard. Despite what you might think, these aren't the graves of unbaptised children (as in some countries), but children under the age of 7 whose parents had no means of paying for an official burial. No more bodies have been accepted since 2008.

TOMB OF THE MARQUIS OF PARANÁ ⑫

Cemitério São João Batista
Rua General Polidoro, Botafogo
• Open daily 9am–5pm
• Admission free • Free monthly guided tours are also available
• Tel: (21) 2539-9449 / 2527-0648 / 2539-6057
• E-mail: saojoaobatista@riopax.com.br
• Reservations at www.cemeteriosjb.com.br/agendamento/
• Metro: Botafogo

> ### Esoteric Egyptian tomb of a Carioca Freemason

Just to the left as you face the cemetery church, the hand of a female statue points to an inscription above the entrance to the esoteric burial chamber of the Marquis and Baron of Paraná.

A politician, diplomat and magistrate known for his conciliatory talents, Honório Hermeto Carneiro Leão, future Marquis of Paraná (1801–1856), was above all a Freemason with a high degree in the Grand Orient of Brazil Lodge. While still a student at the University of Coimbra, Portugal, he had joined a secret society called A Gruta (The Den), founded by Brazilian students with the primary goal of changing Brazil from a monarchy to a republic.

The historic relationship between Freemasonry and the Egyptian tradition is evident here: the vault is shaped like an Egyptian temple and evokes the initiatory mysteries in which the three sides of the pyramid express the elevation of the soul to heaven by invoking the three Masonic tools of compass, set square and sacred book.

The Marquis of Paraná lies here, embalmed by Dr Peixoto, who followed the Sucquet embalming method in the Egyptian tradition, as requested by the deceased. The arrangement of the coffin is also similar to the practice in ancient Egypt: the embalmed corpse was placed in a sealed lead coffin, which was first placed in a varnished cedar coffin. The second coffin was in turn placed inside another magnificent coffin, donated by the brotherhood of the Santa Casa da Misericórdia do Rio de Janeiro (Holy House of Mercy), which ran the necropolis. Three coffins for one body, symbol of the three vital principles animating this mortal coil: the mind, the psyche and the physical.

The female statue attired like an Egyptian priestess, who is facing the tomb and pointing to the inscription above the door, represents immortality rather than death. This is shown by the Sun resplendent on her forehead, a symbol of the god Ra, allegory of spiritual enlightenment, and especially the ankh crosses engraved on her robes with the letter A, initial of *ankh* (ancient Egyptian hieroglyph signifying "life"), representing the consciousness of immortality through Masonic initiation.

At the sides of the inscription are two hawks with acacia leaves in their beaks – the Masonic flower symbolises initiation and immortality and the birds express the winged "soul" of the initiate, who returns to the eternal Orient having been absorbed by the Great Architect of the Universe.

The engravings of women playing the zither represent Nut, goddess of the Sky, wife of Geb (god of the Earth, protector of the dead), and are the allegory of supreme wisdom suggested by the expressive music of universal harmony.

On the ledge above the door is the *uraeus* (serpent), the eye of Horus, god of divine wisdom and spiritual kingship, indicated by the royal serpents (Najas) surrounding the winged Sun. It is the Sun that transmits the vital fluid, the breath of life, which is why the ancient pharaohs wore the rearing *uraeus* on their crowns. The royal serpents should be interpreted as beings that repel evil and therefore protect the funerary monuments and their occupants, reinforced by the presence of Horus, son of Osiris and Isis (the Egyptian Trinity), which eternally fights the forces of darkness for the victory of the forces of light, that is, for immortality to succeed death.

Further protection is given by the sphinx opposite the female statue, placed beside an entrance to the chamber to keep out strangers. In the passive position, the sphinx contemplating the single point on the horizon where the Sun rises was considered the guardian of forbidden entrances and royal mummies. It is the representation of the divine mysteries that surround death and survive the hazards of the cycles of human existence.

STAINED-GLASS WINDOW COMMEMORATING THE NAVY DEAD

Cemitério São João Batista is like an open-air museum – the headstones range from eclectic to neo-Gothic and from Art Deco to neoclassical or modernist. In addition to individual and family graves, such as number 24013 belonging to composer Tom Jobim (1927–1994) or the imposing tomb (133-E) of the "father of aviation", Alberto Santos-Dumont (1873–1932), there are the impressive monuments of the Acadêmia Braziliera de Letras (section 29, 1778-E) and of the military authorities. The tomb commemorating the Mortos da Divisão Naval (behind vault 19970 in avenue 1) is well worth a look. The work of sculptor Leão Velloso (1899–1966), it has an Art Deco exterior and, inside, a magnificent abstract stained-glass window and two statues with a meditative air (see photo).

BRAZIL'S FIRST ABSTRACT SCULPTURE

Through the main entrance of São João Batista cemetery in Rua General Polidoro, to the left before the small office building, you'll discover what is considered to be the first abstract sculpture in Brazil. This anthropomorphic statue with its very simple lines, made from a block of Carrara marble and bronze, represents geologist Orville Adelbert Derby (1851–1915). This is probably the most important work in the cemetery, artistically speaking, because it dates from the early 20th century, at a time when other styles predominated. The work is by the distinguished sculptor Rodolfo Bernardelli, who died in 1931 and was laid to rest in São João Batista's avenue 109-E, known as the "Vieira Souto" of the cemetery – an allusion to the sought-after beachside avenue of that name at Ipanema. Bernardelli himself requested that a beautiful neoclassical bronze sculpture he made in 1879 (when studying in Rome) should be placed on his tomb. It depicts the stoning of Stephen, the first Christian martyr.

The most visited tomb is that of *música popular brasileira* singer Clara Nunes (1942–1983), who is venerated like a saint. People make offerings to her in thanks for pardons received.

CHAPEL ONLY OPEN FOR MASS ON MONDAYS AND THE DAY OF THE DEAD

At the far end of the main avenue is a chapel dating from the time of Dom Pedro II. This very simple little sanctuary only opens for mass on Mondays at 9am and on the Dia de Finados (Day of the Dead, 2 November). A Mass for the first burial in the cemetery was celebrated here on 4 December 1852, a few months after the land was acquired. It was for Rosaura, a slave girl aged 4, as none of the families of the local elite wished to "inaugurate" the cemetery.

Thanks to the many celebrities buried here, including nine former Presidents of the Republic, the cemetery has star quality. The money to purchase the land came from the sale of titles of nobility. Today, through new acquisitions, the total area of 183,000 m² has over 50,000 graves: Christians, other religions (there are more Jews buried here than in the Jewish cemetery at Vila Rosali) and atheists.

PALÁCIO SÃO CLEMENTE, RESIDENCE OF THE CONSUL OF PORTUGAL

⑭

424–466 Rua São Clemente
Botafogo
• Open: last Saturday of each month at 6pm for a public concert
• Free entry
• At 6pm on the last Saturday of each month you can discover the
spectacular São Clemente Palace, the residence of the Consul of Portugal

> *A spectacular palace built in the 1950s*

Although the architectural style of the palace recalls the sumptuous mansions of 18th-century Portugal, the building actually dates from the 1950s and was intended as the Portuguese Embassy.

The building served its purpose for just ten years; in 1960, when the seat of government moved to Brasília, to the detriment of Rio, the palace became the residence of the Consul of Portugal.

Covering an area of 5,800m², the palace was designed by Portuguese architect Guilherme Rebelo de Andrade (1891–1969) and reprises many cultural elements of his homeland, such as the *azulejos* at the main entrance (made in Lisbon by Fábrica de Cerâmica da Viúva Lamego – see *Secret Lisbon* in this series of guides). It also houses a 17th-century Baroque chapel brought over from Portugal (not open to the public during concerts).

The pretty ceramic fountain in front of the entrance is the work of Jorge Barradas (1894–1971).

MUSEU DO MEMORIAL DA PEDIATRIA BRASILEIRA ⑮

381 Rua Cosme Velho
Cosme Velho
• Open Monday to Friday 9am–4pm
• Admission free
• Tel: (21) 2245-3110
• www.sbp.com.br

> **A museum in the heart of the forest**

The Brazilian Pediatrics Memorial Museum is discreetly installed in an attractive colonial house dating from the first half of the 19th century. It is not far from Corcovado train station and just to the right of Bica da Rainha, the fountain where Queen Carlota Joaquina, Dom João VI's wife, came to treat her skin problems. The building was purchased in 1937 by Adehrbal Pougy, one of the engineers who worked on the nearby Rebouças tunnel. This wonderful and friendly little museum is doubly attractive as you can learn more about the history of pediatrics in Brazil but, if that's not for you, just enjoy an unspoilt corner hidden in the heart of Cosme Velho.

Ring the bell at the gate that opens onto the steps leading to the museum itself, surrounded by exuberant gardens. Don't forget to walk round to the terrace at the back, from where there's a stunning view of three private houses overlooking the museum. These prosperous structures in the middle of nowhere include a remarkable "Swiss chalet"; the yellow house just above used to be a necklace workshop.

In front of the museum entrance, on the right, you'll notice a chilling metallic artificial respirator, or iron lung, ancestor of the incubator. Known as the Emerson Respirator, it was made in 1920 by the Massachusetts company of J.H. Emerson and belonged to Rio's Hospital Municipal Jesus.

Inside the museum itself, with its pleasing mix of videos, texts and

contemporary artefacts, don't miss the reproduction of a foundlings' wheel (see p. 167), used for discreetly abandoning unwanted infants at the door of a monastery or *santa casa*.

On the way out of the museum, there's an unrestricted view of a beautiful colonial house with terrace, lost among the greenery, which is now home to a Taoist temple.

PROJETO MORRINHO

Pereirão *favela*
Laranjeiras
• Visits on reservation – Cilan Oliveira will pick you up at the entrance to the *favela* (access from Santa Teresa or Laranjeiras)
• Tel: (21) 7755-6928 / 98308-6298 / 96802-5844
• E-mail: cilanoliveira@hotmail.com

Work of art in a favela

I n the Pereirão *favela* above Laranjeiras district, not far from Rio's French high school, the Morrinho ("small hill" in Portuguese, and by extension "small *favela*" in Rio) project is practically unknown to Cariocas.

It has, however, been showcased around the world – at the 52nd Venice Biennale in 2007 and at New York's MoMA in 2009, as well as the Museu de Arte do Rio (MAR), which shows the project's trademark: miniature reproductions of *favela* life, whose architecture, violence and topography intrigue the world.

It all started in 1997: Cilan Oliveira was 15 when he arrived in Pereirão. To relieve his boredom, he reconstructed the streets and buildings before his eyes with the materials to hand: bricks and earth.

The model grew so realistic that the police dealing with gang warfare took the emerging work of art as a miniature plan of the *favela*. They suspected it was designed to plan drug or arms traffickers' escape routes during military clean-up operations. The artists protested and eventually convinced the authorities of their innocence, while their model narrowly avoided destruction.

In 2002, two filmmakers lifted the project out of anonymity in a popular documentary. The international exhibitions held between 2004 and 2009 came along like a fairy tale, with all the excesses of the art market.

Requests to show their work are fewer nowadays, although still regular, and the Morrinho project has expanded in four areas: film-making, social change projects, travelling exhibitions and tourism. As for Oliveira: "I'll have succeeded when young people, after their experience here, can make a living from their art without our help."

The installation, which nowadays can be toured by calling in advance, is constantly changing, just like the *favela* itself – monumental and fragile at the same time, it has to be repaired after each rainstorm.

SOCIEDADE BUDISTA DO BRASIL ⑰

45 Estrada Dom Joaquim Mamede
Santa Teresa
• Meditation every day except Sunday at 6pm
• Sunday: meditation and teaching around 4.30pm–6.30pm
• Thursday: study group 5pm
• Option of silent spiritual retreats
• Tel: (21) 2245-4331 • sbbcursos@gmail.com
• www.sociedadebudistadobrasil.org

Buddhists in Santa Teresa

You don't just stumble upon the site of the Buddhist Society of Brazil. And even in passing, it's easy to miss.

To find the centre, from Rua Almirante Alexandrino take Estrada Dom Joaquim Mamede, which connects Santa Teresa to the city centre, through Estrada do Sumaré.

About 500 m further along on the left you'll see a flight of steps, covered with drawings and inscriptions announcing the site, leading to the forest. Leave the car and climb the hundred or so steps that lead to the centre itself. It was officially founded in 1967 by members of the Theosophical Society of Brazil.

The centre specialises in the teaching and practice of Theravāda, the oldest branch of Buddhism, practised mainly in Sri Lanka, Thailand, Myanmar, Cambodia and Lao PDR.

It opens regularly for members and occasional visitors, meditation and teaching – an excellent opportunity to try meditation or learn more about Buddhism. Although strictly speaking there isn't a Buddhist monk running the

centre or living there permanently, monks from around the world regularly stay for a few months.

The meditation sessions – there were around thirty participants during our visit – take place on the roof of a building, with a fine view of the neighbourhood.

Interestingly, the Cristo Redentor at Corcovado as seen from the meditation site seems to be blessing the centre, in a fine example of religious syncretism. For some people, Jesus is indeed an avatar (manifestation) of the divine principle, as are Muhammad, Zoroaster, Buddha and Krishna.

FORMER VATICAN EMBASSY IN RIO

Centro Educacional Anísio Teixeira
4098 Rua Almirante Alexandrino
Santa Teresa
• http://www.ceat.org.br/

> *A palace directly inspired by the Palazzo Vecchio in Florence*

The building at the corner of Rua Almirante Alexandrino and Rua Dom Joaquim Mamede looks like a Florentine palace. Dating from 1942, the former Vatican Embassy is now occupied by the Centro Educacional Anísio Teixeira (CEAT).

The banker Oscar Sant'Anna fell in love with the Palazzo Vecchio during a trip to Italy and photographed it from every angle. Back in Rio, he asked architect Faro Filho to build him a palace inspired by his pictures. The tower does indeed closely resemble that of its Florentine ancestor (see photos).

The family then sold the palace to the Vatican. A chapel was added and the papal embassy established there until 1960, when the capital was moved from Rio to Brasilia. Note the papal arms on the stained-glass window in the church.

Some of the house names in the alley just behind CEAT also evoke its former owner: Villa Graças a Deus, Villa Santa Ephigenia, Villa S. Gabriel.

CAMINHO DO GRAFITE

Favela dos Prazeres, Santa Teresa
Casarão dos Prazeres, 3286 Rua Almirante Alexandrino
• Santa Prazeres Tour: (21) 99104-7452 / 96435-9998
• Tours in Portuguese, English or French can be organised daily with community guides
• Admission R$40 per person
• Bus: 507, 014, 007, 006

> *Urban art, breathtaking views and community development*

The Caminho do Grafite (Graffiti Pathway), inaugurated in February 2014, is a permanent exhibition of about eighty murals painted on Morro dos Prazeres houses by forty graffiti artists from the community and elsewhere. The scheme is coordinated by the project manager, Marcio Swk, a local resident and renowned graffiti artist. The trail takes at least an hour and is a good way to explore a Carioca *favela*.

The meeting point is at the entrance to the *favela*, in front of what is now known as Casarão dos Prazeres, a large early 20th-century building that originally belonged to a German family and now houses a school. Long abandoned, it has now been restored and converted into an art and education centre for the local people.

The tour begins up a flight of steps decorated by lines from a poem. Next you come to the first highlight of the visit, the "Dona Branca space", a former landfill site transformed into a small garden with fruit trees, vegetables and medicinal plants. It is looked after by Dona Branca, who lives next door. Nearby, in an explosion of colour, graffiti of all sizes, shapes and inspirations appear. Emerging onto Praça Doce Mel, multiple vistas of the city open out, including a close-up of Cristo Redentor (Christ the Redeemer), with the Pão de Açúcar (Sugar Loaf) virtually opposite and Botafogo bay below. On the other side, you'll see more *favelas*, downtown Rio, the Rio-Niterói bridge across Guanabara bay, and the Zona Norte. In the distance rises Dedo de Deus (Finger of God), a mountain peak in Teresópolis district.

The Graffiti Pathway also offers a semi-wild experience. Over some 300 m towards the top of the hill, you'll pass through dense forest, sometimes with toucans for company. At the top, another surprise: a football pitch with an all-round view of the city. Beyond the field, looking straight ahead, is Tijuca forest with its creeping real estate. On the way down, the trail passes at least two other viewpoints. One of them was a run-down area littered with rubbish before the community transformed it into the Prazeres garden.

The population of the hillside *favelas* of Prazeres and Escondidinho is estimated at 7,000. Since February 2011, the two *favelas* have relied on the constant presence of the Police Pacification Unit (UPP) to keep the peace.

RUSSIAN ORTHODOX CHURCH OF ST ZINAIDA ⑳

210 Rua Monte Alegre
Santa Teresa
• Open Sunday around 9am–11.30am
• Mass Sunday 10am
• Tel: (21) 2252-1471
• http://www.zinaida.orthodoxy.ru

From Russia to Rio

Not far from the Benjamin Constant House Museum, a little further down Rua Monte Alegre, onion-shaped golden domes attract the attention of curious passers-by. Santa Teresa's Russian Orthodox church, open only on Sunday mornings (just push open the door that looks closed), was built in 1927 by White Russians fleeing the Bolshevik Revolution. The Santa Teresa neighbourhood was chosen because many affluent Russians and Brazilians lived there: the district had prospered from 1850 because of its altitude, as yellow-fever carrying mosquitoes were much less of a problem.

Note that as in most Orthodox churches, you can't sit down and enjoy the atmosphere, the chanting and the iconostasis that separates the priest from the worshippers.

The church owes its name to the fact that the wife of the architect, Gleb Konstantinovich Sakharov, was called Zinaida. St Zinaida was a member of St Paul's family. The name means "of the family of Zeus" or "divine girl".

The first Russians arrived in Brazil in the late 19th century, mainly in Rio Grande do Sul, to cultivate the land.

NEARBY

THE REMAINS OF THE SANTA TERESA CABLE CAR ㉑

Museu Casa de Benjamin Constant
255 Rua Monte Alegre
Santa Teresa
• Open Wednesday to Friday 1pm–5pm, weekends 10am–5pm
• Tel: (21) 3970-1177 / 3970-1168

At the bottom left of the garden of the Benjamin Constant House Museum, you'll notice two circular holes in the wall. They were for the cables of the car that connected Rua de Matacavalos (old name for Rua Riachuelo) to the terminal at Largo do Guimarães, passing by the current museum. Inaugurated in 1877, the cable car was operated by a steam engine until 1894, at the same time as the celebrated Santa Teresa tramway. Designed by engineer Jánurio Cândido de Oliveira, it extended over 513 m and three viaducts had to be constructed for it. The first station was at 89 Travessa do Castro.

FOUNDLINGS' WHEELS, CARMELITE CONVENTO DE SANTA TERESA

㉒

52 Ladeira de Santa Teresa
Santa Teresa
• Open Monday to Friday 6am–12 noon and 2pm–5pm, Saturday and
Sunday closes 4pm

> *How to abandon your child discreetly*

Although there are several reproductions of foundlings' wheels in Rio (see opposite), those at Santa Teresa convent are the only ones still at their original site. These wooden wheels were used to abandon babies discreetly (see opposite). The two examples at the convent are in the sacristy, one to the right of the church, the other in the room to the left of the sanctuary, which also has some lovely *azulejos*.

You'll see in both of them that the space at the bottom where you could leave your child is relatively narrow, to stop older children being abandoned ... The top part of these wheels was also used (and still is today) as a means of communication between the cloistered sisters and the rest of the world, without them having to speak or be seen.

The first foundlings' wheel in Brazil was installed in El Salvador in 1726. In the second half of the 19th century, there were up to fourteen of them in the country. The last working example, removed in 1949, was in São Paulo. In Rio, they were in operation from 1738 for two hundred years until abolished under legislation on minors in 1938.

A reproduction of a foundlings' wheel can be seen at the museum of the Brazilian Historical and Geographical Institute (see p. 122), another at the Brazilian Pediatrics Memorial Museum at Cosme Velho (see p. 157) and a third at the Educandário (boarding school) Romão de Mattos Duarte (60 Rua Paulo VI, Flamengo), although the latter isn't on permanent display.

The House of the Wheel, later called the Foundlings' House and now Romão de Mattos Duarte boarding school in homage to its founder, was located next to the hospital of Santa Casa da Misericórdia, at Castelo, between 1738 and 1821. It moved several times, until settling at Flamengo in a large house built in 1911 on land that belonged to the Comte d'Eu, husband of Princess Isabel.

ABANDONING YOUR CHILD: A WAY OF FREEING BLACK BABIES FROM SLAVERY

In the 18th and 19th centuries, an estimated 10 per cent of Brazil's newborns were abandoned as a result of poverty among the working classes or to protect the reputation of upper-class women who had an illegitimate child. The wheels were also seen as a chance to free black babies from slavery – some slaves left a child there for that reason alone.

WHAT IS A FOUNDLINGS' WHEEL?

It is said that in 787, Dateus, a priest in Milan, began placing a large basket outside his church so that abandoned infants could be left there. More organised initiatives for the reception of abandoned children were begun by the Hospice des Chanoines in Marseilles from 1188 onwards, with Pope Innocent III (1198-1216) later giving the practice the Church's benediction; he had been horrified by the terrible sight of the bodies of abandoned infants floating in the Tiber and was determined to do something to save them.

So the doors of convents were equipped with a sort of rotating cradle which made it possible for parents to leave their infant anonymously and without exposing it to the elements. The infant was left in the outside section of the cradle, and then the parent rang a bell so that the nuns could activate the mechanism and bring the child inside. Access to the "turntable" was, however, protected by a grille so narrow that only newborn infants would fit through...

Abandoned during the 19th century, the system had to be readopted after some twenty years at various places in Europe due to the sharp upturn in the number of infants abandoned.

ACADEMIA BRASILEIRA DE LITERATURA DE CORDEL ㉓

37 Rua Leopoldo Fróes
Santa Teresa
• Open daily 9am–5.59pm when Gonçalo isn't travelling
• Tel: (21) 2232-4801 / 2221-1077

> *Popular culture in academic rhymes*

A short distance from Getulio Damaso's curious "tram-shaped" workshop where he recycles scrap materials, the Brazilian Academy of Cordel Literature was founded by Gonçalo Ferreira da Silva. He still runs it today.

The *cordel* – a booklet of "stories on a string" that has survived in Brazil and Portugal as well as some other European countries – is a collection of short texts in verse, intended to inform the non-reading public who wouldn't buy an "expensive and time-consuming" book.

The *cordels* deal with many subjects: news items, recent and ancient history, social phenomena, political analysis, economic, scientific or biographical – all the names that have left their mark on the world, from Gandhi to Mao Zedong, Laplace to Archimedes.

Gonçalo Ferreira da Silva was born in 1937 in Ipu, in the state of Ceara. His mother couldn't read at all, his father barely. He learned something of life through the kindness of neighbours but, having known poverty, at the age of

14 he lied about his age to go to Rio de Janeiro. After months of wandering and sleeping rough, he got to know the troubadours or *cordelistes*: he went to their meetings, where verbal jousting stimulated the search for a good rhyme, the right word, the accuracy of an idea. They all shared a deep knowledge of the Portuguese language. Gonçalo published his first booklet in 1978 and, with six other people, founded the academy on 7 September 1988. There are currently forty of these lovers of their beautiful language, of wordplay and good humour. All of them bear in mind the motto *produzir, preservar, divulgar* (produce, preserve, disclose). Their mission is limitless: offering modest people the opportunity to experience the world through the written word.

If you visit 37 Rua Leopoldo Fróes, you can buy a *cordel* (in several languages, for R$2 a copy) and chat with Gonçalo (in Portuguese). If much of his recitation of the legend of the *uirapuru* (the bird that sings only once a year and whose song commands total silence in the Amazon forest) is incomprehensible, don't worry: just savouring these rhymes that bounce back and forth is still a great treat.

WHERE DOES THE WORD "*CORDEL*" COME FROM?

Cordel comes from the practice of offering the booklets hanging from strings like washing in the wind, held up by clothes pegs. It was a cheap way of displaying many copies in a small space. The illustrations in these booklets are monochrome woodcuts, engraved by various artists in a simple but expressive style.

COPACABANA
URCA

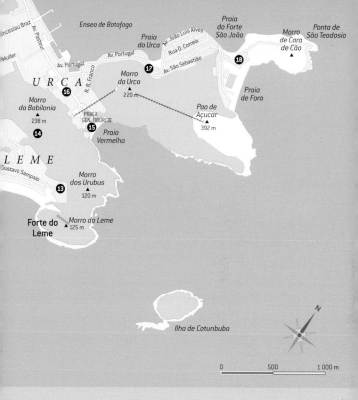

NAPOLEON'S LOCK OF HAIR ❶

Museu Histórico do Exército
Forte de Copacabana
1 Praça Coronel Eugênio Franco (end of Avenida Atlântica, posto VI)
• www.fortedecopacabana.com
• Open Tuesday to Sunday 10am–8pm
• Admission: adults R$6, over 60s and students R$3, free for children
under 10, over 80s and members of the armed forces
• Metro: Praça General Osório • Bus: 121, 126, 127, 484, 455

> **What's
> a lock
> of Napoleon's hair
> doing in Rio?**

Who'd have imagined that a lock of the French Emperor's hair would be displayed in a Rio museum? It's easy to miss in the "Gallery of Curiosities" of the Historical Museum of the Army, despite sitting next to a small bust and statue of Napoleon Bonaparte.

This lock of hair was donated in 1992 by the family of Marshal Castelo Branco (first President of Brazil after the 1964 military coup d'état), after his death.

Although a short note in French in the glass case simply indicates that the lock was obtained after the Emperor died, the archives are slightly more revealing.

Three weeks before his death, Napoleon dictated his will to his valet, Marchand. Among other instructions, he wanted his hair cut off after his death so that locks of it could be added to gold bracelets that were to be given to his mother and brothers.

Marchand respected Napoleon's instructions and cut his hair on two occasions after his death. The first time, he only cut the hair from the top of the skull and the body was displayed wearing a hat during the funeral ceremony. The rest of the hair was cut just before burial.

We don't, however, know how many locks of hair were taken, or how they were distributed beyond those stipulated in the will, or why Marshal Castelo Branco's family came into possession of one of them.

PAVEMENT DEDICATED TO CARLOS DRUMMOND DE ANDRADE

Largo do Poeta
Junction of Avenida Rainha Elisabeth and Rua
Conselheiro Lafaiete
• Metro: General Osório

Famous poet next door

At the junction of Avenida Rainha Elisabeth and Rua Conselheiro Lafaiete, known as Largo do Poeta (Poet's Plaza), it's easy to miss the Portuguese texts inscribed at the four corners of the pavement. These are excerpts from four poems by Carlos Drummond de Andrade (1902–1987), a leading Brazilian poet who lived nearby, at number 60 Rua Conselheiro Lafaiete:

Ó vida futura nós te criaremos ("Oh future life we will create you" – from the poem *Mundo grande*)

E agora José ("And now José" – *José*)

Vontade de cantar mas tão absoluta que me calo repleto ("The will to sing but so absolute that I am silenced satisfied" – *Canto esponjoso*)

Toda história é remorso ("All history is remorse" – *Claro enigma*)

Largo do Poeta, Rio's posthumous tribute to the writer from Minas Gerais, was inaugurated in August 1990. Andrade, a widely published poet and journalist, was also principal private secretary to the Minister of Education, Gustavo Capanema. The painting *Água* (Water), from the abstract series by Cândido Portinari, hangs in his office at the former ministry headquarters, now known as Palácio Gustavo Capanema (see p. 48).

Andrade loved to walk around the neighbourhood and regularly strolled down Avenida Rainha Elisabeth to the beach. There, facing the ocean at Copacabana, his famous bronze statue is seated on a bench along the promenade.

MOSAIC BY LYGIA CLARK ❸

3392 Avenida Atlântica

The first steps of a great artist

At the entrance to the residential building at number 3992 Avenida Atlântica, between Avenida Rainha Elisabeth and Rua Julio de Castilhos, a genuine forgotten treasure of Brazilian contemporary art can be seen from the pavement: a multicoloured mosaic depicting the human body and various abstract shapes. The work mentions the year 1951 in its bottom right corner, beside the signature of Lygia Clark, one of Brazil's most important artists. Art lovers will enjoy the challenge of trying to identify, in this work by someone who was in the process of becoming a painter and sculptor, the early stages of the body of great work produced by Lygia Clark. A revolutionary artist who described herself as a "non-artist", Clark destroyed paradigms and broke away from the limits of formal art. In 1954, for example, she was already incorporating the frame into her works as a physical element.

Lygia Clark, one of the founders of Neoconcretism, was born in Belo Horizonte in the state of Minas Gerais in 1920 and died in Rio de Janeiro in 1988. She moved gradually from two- to three-dimensional art and in 1960 created the *Bichos*, structures made from metal sheets, which invite the observer to handle them.

She subsequently continued to explore the senses, investigated bodily experiences and concentrated on the therapeutic possibilities of sensory art. This all led her, towards the end of her life, to see her work as being closer to psychoanalysis. Clark's work has received international recognition and major museums throughout the world have held retrospectives devoted to her. Her work achieved record sums for a Brazilian artist in 2013 in auctions held in Brazil and abroad.

Such is the importance of the *Bichos* in Lygia Clark's work that in 2015, to celebrate the 95th anniversary of her birth, Google paid homage to her with a special Doodle depicting the *Bichos*.

TO LIVE HAPPILY, LIVE HIDDEN

Long-standing residents of the street who use the library today claim that the house has no windows because the owner didn't want passers-by to see the goings-on inside. The remains of the wall in the little garden next to the street seem to confirm this version of events: in other words, the master of the house asked for a flight of steps leading directly to his bedroom so he could conduct his amorous liaisons discreetly.

BIBLIOTECA ESCOLAR MUNICIPAL DE ❹
COPACABANA CARLOS DRUMMOND DE ANDRADE

80 Rua Sá Ferreira
• Open Monday to Friday 9am–5pm (last entry 4.45pm)
• Admission free
• Metro: Praça General Osório (Sá Ferreira exit)
• Tel: (21) 2267-5561 / 2227-0783

> **The house with no windows**

Wedged in beside Rua Saint Roman, a steep street leading to the Cantagalo-Pavão-Pavãozinho group of *favelas*, the Copacabana Municipal School Library is located in one of the city's most unusual buildings. Thanks to its Art Deco details and overlapping volumes, this is considered the most advanced Brazilian architectural project of the 1920s.

Although the small library, popularly known as "the house with no windows", is meant for children (who call it the "witch's castle"), it welcomes grown-ups as well.

The building, which was listed by the city of Rio in 1996, is officially known as Casa Villiot. Designed by the Italian architect Antonio Virzi (see p. 133), it was the residence of engineer Victor Villiot Martins. When the house was built in 1929, it made such an impression that the President of the Brazilian Republic himself, Washington Luís, paid a visit. This is Virzi's last-known work in Rio.

Half-hidden behind a wall, the house almost waits to be discovered by passers-by. But once inside, its beauty and inventiveness are immediately apparent: despite the lack of windows, a pleasant natural light filters through

many small coloured-glass panels and the two fountains (out of order) in what were once the living and dining rooms.

This two-storey residence was restored in 2006. Although the shelves of books make it difficult to see certain details and interior perspectives, you can still appreciate the corners, curves, angles and decorative hand-painted panels, as well as the superb original lamp fittings. Also look out for the bath, on the second floor near the former bedroom.

IGREJA SANTA CRUZ DE COPACABANA ❺

Shopping Cidade Copacabana (also known as Shopping dos Antiquários or Antiques Mall)
143 Rua Siqueira Campos, 4th floor 2235-3200
• Open daily
• Admission free
• Metro: Siqueira Campos

A modern church on a shopping-centre terrace

The small church of Santa Cruz de Copacabana is hidden away on a sort of wide concrete terrace dotted with a few potted plants, a few metres from the metro station between Siqueira Campos and Figueiredo Magalhães streets. Take the little-used circular ramps in Cidade Copacabana shopping centre as far as the fourth and last floor to find it. The 400 m^2 church has glass walls, and the gently curving concrete roof takes the form of two merging vaults. This gives a feeling of lightness, in contrast to the great mass of the surrounding buildings.

This church with its pared-down decoration was consecrated in July 1961 even before the construction of the mall was completed. Apart from its modernist architecture, it is also worth a visit to see the faithful replica of the Turin Shroud (a length of linen purporting to be the burial garment of Christ) on the wall behind the altar. This silk-screen print was donated to the church

in the early 2000s by the Italian Sindonology Centre (Shroud Studies).

The Cidade Copacabana centre, designed by architects Mindlin & Associados, was one of the first in Rio de Janeiro. It features long corridors and a spiral ramp reminiscent of the one in New York's Guggenheim Museum, very bold for its time, which smoothed the flow of visitors.

PARQUE ESTADUAL DE CHACRINHA

End of Rua Guimarães Natal, between Ladeira do Leme and Rua Assis Brasil
• Open Tuesday to Sunday 8am–5pm
• Admission free
• Metro: Cardeal Arcoverde

Copacabana's hidden park

Strolling through the noisy Rua Barata Ribeiro, the location of Cardeal Arcoverde metro station, you'd never guess that at the end of Rua Guimarães Natal is the entrance to Chacrinha State Park, amid the buildings and hills of São João and Babilônia. This park, one of the last areas with traces of the Atlantic forest in the Zona Sul, has a hiking trail that can be covered in about an hour.

Besides the plant and animal life, the remaining traces throw light on aspects of the history of the neighbourhood and of Rio. In particular, at one end of the path, you'll discover the ruined foundations of the Casa de Teodoro (Teodoro's House). Probably dating from the early 19th century, it was built of stone, clay and shells. It is said to be the oldest residence in Copacabana and is thought to have belonged to a fisherman called Teodoro.

Some of the park's paths were originally trodden by the indigenous people and by the soldiers protecting the city. The "mule path", for example, was opened during the colonial period to transport provisions for the soldiers guarding Rio. You can also see the ruins of the lookout platforms, a shrine, and the aqueduct that carried water collected on the rocky slopes of the hill to a fountain, whose remains are still visible.

Near the entrance to the park (which covers 13.3 hectares) is a recreation and sports area. Some climbers also venture off the historical-natural path.

Although formally established in 1969 as the first city park, it was only about twenty years later that Chacrinha began to fulfil its role of a public space and to assume its nature-preservation mission. Until then, it was occupied by a *favela*, used as landfill and for a samba school.

COPACABANA BATCAVE

❼

Cardeal Arcoverde metro station
Rua Barata Ribeiro, by Rua Rodolfo Dantas
• Open daily during metro operating hours

*Batman
in Rio*

Step onto a platform of Cardeal Arcoverde metro station and you'll think you're in a cave – much of the walls and ceiling seems to be bare rock with a rough cement coating. The same design is found in the corridors on the floor above, where the station's long ventilation shaft rises to the surface. If you stand under the duct and have a good look upwards, however, the legendary Batman logo is lit up.

This unexpected sight is one more example of Carioca humour and irreverence. It all started shortly before the station opened, when an engineer brought his children to see the construction work, joking that this was Batman's cave. The children were excited to hear that but insisted on proof. So one of the engineers thought of attaching the Batman logo to the duct outlet. On their next visit, the children were thrilled: that was what had been missing to confirm Batcave status! After the station opened in June 1998, passengers also grew fond of the local Batman. So much so, according to older employees, that when the logo faded away, the public "demanded" a replacement. The current logo is the third.

A STATION WITH DOZENS OF COPIES OF BRAZILIAN ROCKS

In the station garden on Rua Barata Ribeiro, a large pink boulder sets the scene for what lies inside. Unlike all Rio's other stations, the floor here is covered with dozens of samples of Brazilian rocks, "formed over 400 million years ago", according to the engraving on a steel door half-hidden on the Zona Norte platform.

Entitled *Embarque na Estação Terra* [Boarding at Earth Station], the text explains the formation of the planet and describes the rocks in these words: "Time and the movements of the Earth are the artists that created the rocks. The inks they used are mixtures of molecules and atoms."

REMAINS OF MORROS DO INHANGÁ   **8**

Avenida Nossa Senhora de Copacabana, next to number 374
• Metro: Cardeal Arcoverde

> *The flight
> of steps
> that divides
> the avenue in two*

Between 374 Avenida Nossa Senhora de Copacabana and Sala Baden Powell is a long flight of seventy-five steps; they follow the remains of the former Morros do Inhangá, which divided Avenida Nossa Senhora de Copacabana. The steps end at Rua General Barbosa Lima, a residential street of apartments and houses. Rua General Azevedo Pimentel, a quiet little street that is actually a dead end, runs from the other side of the *morro* to Avenida Barata Ribeiro, opposite Praça Cardeal Arcoverde. There is another flight of seventy-seven steps leading to the top of the hill. The walk gives you an idea of the transformation Copacabana has undergone.

Until the 1920s, one of the three *morros* was behind one side of the famous Copacabana Palace Hotel. The hill was excavated to build Avenida Nossa Senhora de Copacabana, then divided, to become one long boulevard of 3.2 km. In 1934, another little hill was wiped off the map to construct the pool at Copacabana Palace (until Avenida Atlântica was opened in 1906, this hill cut the beach in two at high tide). Whatever still remained in 1951 was demolished to make way for the Chopin, Balada and Prelúdio buildings next to the hotel.

There are also remains of this last section of the *morro* behind the buildings between Rua Fernando Mendes and Rua Republica do Peru. You can gather some idea of how it used to look from the patio of Pedro Alvares Cabral college.

Inhangá comes from *Anhangá*, a word of Tupí-Guaraní origin meaning "evil spirit", "wandering soul" or "spirit that wanders". The name seems to have come about because the rocky slopes of the *morro* attracted lightning during storms.

Copacabana Palace Hotel, listed as national heritage, was built to receive visitors to the International Exposition celebrating the centenary of Brazilian independence from Portugal in 1922 (see p. 54).
However, it only opened in 1923 due to contractors' delays and violent storm damage to the lower floors in 1922. Despite none of the scenes being filmed there, the hotel inspired the Hollywood musical *Flying Down to Rio*, when Fred Astaire and Ginger Rogers danced together for the first time. The whole thing was shot in Hollywood studio sets reproducing parts of the hotel.

ITAHY BUILDING

252 Avenida Nossa Senhora de Copacabana
• Metro: Cardeal Arcoverde

> **The symbol of Art Deco native to Rio**

I f there is one Rio building that symbolises local Art Deco and represents the indigenous influence on Brazilian Modernismo, it has to be the Itahy, at 252 Avenida Nossa Senhora de Copacabana.

The building was designed in 1932 by Arnaldo Gladosch. This São Paulo architect, the son of German immigrants, trained in Europe in 1926 at the Königlich-Sächsisches Polytechnikum (Royal Saxon Polytechnic Institute). The Itahy blends different references, its entrance topped by a spectacular "Indian-mermaid-caryatid" and the sleek aerodynamic lines of refined Art Deco architecture in the body of the building.

Pedro Correia de Araújo, who was responsible for the decoration of the portico and lobby, was born in Paris and lived there until the 1920s. He came from a noble family from Pernambuco (old and trusted friends of Emperor Dom Pedro II, who emigrated to Paris with him when he went into exile after the proclamation of the Republic in 1889). Correia de Araújo knew Picasso, Léger and Matisse, among others, while he was at the Académie Ranson (an art school founded by French painter Paul Ranson).

Correia de Araújo returned to Brazil with nativist ideas, influenced by artist Ivan da Silva Bruhns, another Brazilian living in Paris and one of the most important exponents of the art of tapestry. Seeing Brazil from afar let them appreciate how an individual style could spring from their own background.

The cylindrical ceramic pieces that frame the entrance to the building show the influence of the Printemps department store's design studio at the 1925 International Exposition of Modern Decorative and Industrial Arts in Paris. The entrance door of hammered metal is ornamented with images of seaweed and turtles. Inside the hall, a tiled floor features ocean waves. The walls have relief carvings of fish and other marine symbols.

In the neighbouring district of Leme, Rua Gustavo Sampaio, the Manguaba building also features decorative art by Pedro Correia de Araújo. Similar aerodynamic architecture (by Chaves & Campelo, 1936) highlights the marriage between nativism and modernism. Ceramic panels at the entrance, majolica columns ... all lead back to the Itahy.

RIO DE JANEIRO, CAPITAL OF LATIN AMERICAN ART DECO

The city of Rio de Janeiro has over 400 significant Art Deco buildings, including the largest monument of its kind, the Cristo Redentor (Christ the Redeemer) at Corcovado. At least 200 of these would be worthy of inclusion in any collection dedicated to the movement.

Carioca Art Deco developed over the period 1920 to 1950. Its heyday coincided with the government of Getúlio Vargas, in particular during the dictatorship of the Estado Novo (New State) from 1937 to 1945. Vargas wanted to show Rio de Janeiro to the world as the symbol of a new Brazil, a showcase of modernity and global potential, and the universal architectural language of 1930s avant-garde was Art Deco.

Some government buildings of the time, like those of the Ministries of War, Labour and Finance, are icons of the genre.

The majority of official buildings – post offices, airports, the Central do Brasil railway station (along with the Ministry of War, the station forms the largest Art Deco district in Latin America), state schools – adopted the Art Deco style, both in its historical references and its streamlined aerodynamics.

Whereas in Europe, the First and Second World Wars had made all tourism impossible between 1914 and 1918 and 1939 and 1945 (respectively, the gestation period and apogee of Art Deco), Rio de Janeiro had become an ideal tourist destination. And much more: European stocks of Art Deco objects, furniture, artworks in general, were widely collected in South America. Brazilian ships left home with the raw materials for war or essentials such as iron, rubber, chocolate and coffee, and returned from Europe laden with crystal, porcelain and bronzes ...

If we had to date the high point of Carioca Art Deco, we'd highlight the two cruises to the Rio Carnaval in 1938 and 1939 of the French transatlantic liner *Normandie* (the largest, most modern and luxurious of its time), organised by Boston agent Raymond Whitcomb. During the North Atlantic winter, there were no passengers on the *Normandie*'s usual route (Le Havre–Southampton–New York). Seizing the opportunity, Whitcomb hired the liner and managed to fully book it right away. Some of the Art Deco cabins, of various designs, cost the equivalent of US$130,000.

On arrival at Guanabara, the immense size of the *Normandie* meant that it had to anchor in Botafogo bay rather than tie up in port. The liner was transformed into a real spectacle, lit up at night and open to the public by day. Visitor tickets could be purchased at the office of the Compagnie Générale Transatlantique.

Today, Rio de Janeiro is the undisputed Art Deco capital of Latin America: in 1996, at the first international seminar of Art Deco in Latin America, more than 500 participants paid tribute to this cultural heritage.

In 2011, the 11th World Congress on Art Deco was organised in Rio by the International Coalition of Art Deco Societies (ICADS) and Brazil's Art Deco Institute (the pioneering society founded in 2005) – the first time the congress had been held in a Latin American country.

ITAÓCA BUILDING ❿

43 Rua Duvivier
Copacabana
• Metro: Cardeal Arcoverde

An Art Deco amulet?

One of the first buildings of over ten storeys in Copacabana – Itaóca, at 43 Rua Duvivier – has brought a sophisticated European flair to the neighbourhood. With staff rooms on the top floor, it is for both commercial and residential use, notably the street-level apartments that are the headquarters of the Alliance Française.

Designed in 1928 by architects Anton Floderer and Robert Prentice and built by the Christiano & Nielsen company, the building has a streamlined feel with projecting volumes, rounded corners and horizontal friezes, and a nativist-inspired entrance with striking columns of green majolica.

On these columns, as in the main section of the building, there are elements which reference the Amazonian amulets know as *muiraquitãs* (see box). Perhaps designed by Fernando Correia Dias, the nativist allegories of Itaóca have yet to be investigated. There is, however, no doubt about the building's front door: it comes from the same factory as that of the neighbouring Itahy building (see p. 183).

Inside, flooring with alternating green and yellow lozenges evokes the Brazilian flag. A large interior patio (unusual for Copacabana) supplies the building with ventilation and lighting.

MUIRAQUITÃS: AMAZONIAN AMULETS

The *muiraquitã* is an amulet to which indigenous tribes, mainly Amazonian, attribute magical powers. These amulets might be stone, clay, ceramic or even wood. They take the form of animals such as frogs (as in the entrance to the Itaóca building) or alligators, but also stylised human figures. In Mário de Andrade's novel *Macunaíma* (1928), hailed as the nativist epic of Brazilian Modernismo, the plot develops around the search for a lost *muiraquitã*.

In July 1925, at the Théâtre des Champs-Élysées in Paris, the ballet "Legends, Beliefs and Amulets of the Amazon Indians" – adapted by P.L. Duchartre from images drawn by Brazilian modernist Vicente do Rego Monteiro – was performed to great acclaim. For fifteen days, while the International Exposition of Modern Decorative and Industrial Arts (a World's Fair dedicated to Art Deco) was held in the city, attracting visitors from around the world, the theatre on Avenue Montaigne was always packed.

In Brazil, sculptor Victor Brecheret incorporated Amazonian *muiraquitãs* into various works in bronze, terracotta or marble.

GUAHY BUILDING

⓫

181 Rua Ronald de Carvalho
Lido
Copacabana
• Metro: Cardeal Arcoverde

> **One of Rio's most significant Art Deco buildings**

The Guahy building, a Ricardo Buffa project dating from 1932, is one of the most important Art Deco buildings in Rua Ronald de Carvalho and the Copacabana district.

Guahy, rooted in the "Cubist House" project (see photo) of Raymond Duchamp-Villon (1876–1918), was presented at the Paris Salon d'Automne in 1912 but was never carried through.

If only by its shape, the building also highlights the nativist influences of modern architects: the lines of the balcony railings and the main doorway recall the decorative arts of the Marajoara (indigenous tribes of the Ilha de Marajó, an island near Belém in northern Brazil) and the entrance gate represents their traditional headgear. Not to mention the name Guahy, also of indigenous origin.

Guahy was threatened with demolition in the 1980s after it was purchased by an investor from Minas Gerais who was planning to open a hotel on the site. Thanks to the intervention of Luiz Paulo Conde, planning administrator of Rio de Janeiro at the time, the building was protected and listed, and the purchaser was obliged to restore it instead of knocking it down. Around this period, the process began of preserving the entire Lido district of Copacabana, which has about fifty Art Deco buildings worth restoring and preserving.

Many TV productions, including the Globo network *telenovelas* (soaps), were filmed here, either on site or in studio sets.

Ricardo Buffa is also the architect of one of the most interesting Carioca buildings at 108 Rua Hermenegildo in Barros (Santa Teresa). The entrance is surrounded by Art Deco pillars.

Poet, writer and art critic, Ronald de Carvalho, after whom the street is named, was one of the mentors of Brazilian Modernismo.

ROXY STAIRCASE COPIES OCEAN LINER

The beautiful Art Deco staircase of the Roxy cinema (945A Avenida Nossa Senhora de Copacabana), designed in 1934 by Brazilian architect Raphael Galvão, is a faithful copy of the one in the dining room of *The Atlantic*, an ocean liner that entered into service in 1930.

LOBBY OF EDIFÍCIO PETRÔNIO ⓬

45 Rua Ronald de Carvalho
• Metro: Cardeal Arcoverde

> *A building inspired by a project of Adolf Loos for Josephine Baker?*

Also known as Edifício Almeida Magalhães, the Petrônio building was designed in 1934 by Carlos Porto and Caio Moacyr for the entrepreneur owner Petrônio de Almeida Magalhaes.

This is one of the most remarkable buildings in Copacabana: although its façade echoes the aerodynamic streamlining of its neighbour (see box), the entrance offers superb colour contrasts, using European marbles (Siena yellow and Portoro black) on the walls, the floor and the central column.

These bands of colour are thought to have been inspired by a 1927 project by Austrian architect Adolf Loos (author of the 1908 manifesto *Ornament and Crime*, attacking ornamentation in art), for the home of Josephine Baker, Franco-American muse of Art Deco. Never built – though the plans have been reproduced in various books and exhibitions – the house was meant to be completely covered with black and white stripes, in an obvious reference to the artist's roots and the "white" world of her devoted fans. Baker visited Rio de Janeiro for the first time in 1929 and received a standing ovation at the Cassino Beira Mar theatre.

COPACABANA'S FIRST SKYSCRAPER

The nearby OK building (1928) at the corner of Rua Ronald de Carvalho and Avenida Atlântica, now known as the Ribeiro Moreira building, is considered to be the first skyscraper in Copacabana with its fourteen floors.

OBELISK TO MARK THE WIDENING OF AVENIDA ATLÂNTICA

Praça Júlio de Noronha
Leme
• Metro: Cardeal Arcoverde

A souvenir of 1910 Copacabana

In the farthest reaches of the Leme neighbourhood, a small obelisk in Praça Júlio de Noronha is hardly ever noticed. Yet it commemorates an important fact of Carioca life: the widening of Avenida Atlântica to 12 m in 1910.

Up to that time, the avenue was still quite small: one lane in each direction, two sidewalks, and a central reservation with a few street lights installed together with the obelisk that is now at Leme.

In the 1930s, the central reservation was eliminated and the obelisk, which had stood on Rua Almirante Gonçalves, was transferred to its current location. Unfortunately, it has suffered from vandalism: much of the bronze lettering has disappeared, making it almost impossible to read the inscription.

The avenue only took on its current appearance in the 1970s: under the engineer Hildebrando de Góes Filho, the beach itself was significantly extended and again the avenue was widened. Roberto Burle Marx was commissioned to design the famous waves on the sidewalk (incidentally, he changed the initial direction of the waves to the design we know today).

Although the avenue, with its six lanes, is useful for drivers, it's a nightmare for others: local residents (who can't open their windows because of the deafening noise) or those who'd like a drink at one of the beach bars (it's sometimes difficult to hear your neighbour), not to mention the disappointing quality of the bars and restaurants because of lack of space. Just suppose that, with improved public transport, the avenue could rediscover a human scale (two lanes instead of the current six?). The space gained from the roadway could at last be used to install bars and restaurants worthy of the name, where you could listen to the conversations and the waves instead of the countless buses with their exhaust fumes. As you can at the bars along the Arpoador peninsula ...

HIKING AT MORRO DA BABILÔNIA ⓮

Favela Inn
32 Rua Dr Nelson
Chapéu Mangueira—Leme
• Admission: R$30 to R$40
• Bus: 535, 538, 472, 190 • Tel: (21) 3209-2870 / 99568-4966

> **A fantastic and little-known trail**

The little-known trail in the Environmental Protection Area (APA – Área de Proteção Ambiental) of Morro da Babilônia (Babylon hill), overlooking the *favelas* of Babilônia and Chapéu Mangueira, makes an outstanding walk. From its 200 m peak, the steep ridge offers some magnificent and unusual views of the city: from Corcovado to Sugarloaf Mountain, from Copacabana to Pedra da Gávea, from Botafogo bay and Aterro ("landfill") do Flamengo to Centro and the Zona Norte.

The local residents, organised into cooperatives, have reforested the area and they maintain the trails. The walk takes about three hours. For the start of the itinerary, make your way through the busy streets of Babilônia.

The guide, born and raised in the *favela*, shows you the results of recent reurbanisation: the contrast between the "new", with its exclusive views of the world-famous sands of Praia de Copacabana, and the rustic, almost rural, areas.

Shortly after passing the last houses along the way, you'll go back in time to discover the home of Seu Antônio. This mud hut, where he has lived for seventy-one years, was built by his grandfather in 1902. It offers a striking contrast to today's solidly built housing with its running water and sanitation. Seu Antônio, in his friendly way, might well invite you in.

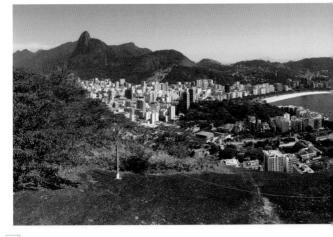

The most significant species of local fauna and flora are identified on boards set along the trail (in English and Portuguese). There are also the ruins of the city's defence system from the colonial era and the Second World War. Since 2009 and the installation of a Police Pacification Unit (UPP – Unidade de Polícia Pacificadora), the *favelas* of Babilônia and Chapéu Mangueira have seen many changes, not always controversy-free, including urban planning schemes and local micro-business initiatives.

MORRO DA BABILÔNIA AT CANNES

Orfeu Negro (Black Orpheus), winner of the 1959 Cannes Film Festival Palme d'Or and an Oscar for Best Foreign Film in 1960, transposes the tragic love story of Orpheus and Eurydice to a Rio *favela* during Carnaval. The score by Tom Jobim and Vinicius de Moraes is one of the references for bossa nova (new beat). The opening and closing scenes with the dying Orpheus and Eurydice, among others, were shot in Pedra do Urubu, near the top of Babylon hill.

Although the Leme neighbourhood was established in 1894, around the same time as Ipanema, Chapéu Mangueira dates from 1889, with shacks that were built at the site of the present-day Forte de Leme. In Rua General Ribeiro da Costa stood the house and first workshop (no longer there) of landscaper Roberto Burle Marx (1909–1994). Strolling up the steep streets of the *favela* to Rua Barroso, you'll also discover the large yellow residence that belonged to the celebrated Brazilian composer Ary Barroso (1903–1964). Among other popular songs, he wrote *Aquarela do Brasil*. The former community leader Benedita da Silva, who was elected councillor, then governor of Rio de Janeiro *estado* (state), also lived in Chapéu Mangueira. Apart from *Orfeu Negro*, other movies and TV soap opera scenes have been filmed in the community, including *Babilônia 2000*, directed by Eduardo Coutinho.

STATUE OF CHOPIN

Praia Vermelha

Chopin confiscated

During the Nazi invasion of Poland in 1939, Polish radio insistently broadcast Chopin's *Polonaise* (Opus 40) to keep up the people's patriotic spirit. This is why the Germans, when they took over the country, destroyed the composer's statue in Warsaw. In response, Polish expatriates in Rio commissioned a statue of Chopin from August Zamoysky, who lived in the city from 1938 to 1955. The statue was delivered in 1944 and installed in Praça General Tibúrcio, in Urca. In 1951 the mayor of Rio, Mendes de Morais, asked for it to be moved in front of the Teatro Municipal (see opposite) but at every Carnaval, Chopin found himself decorated with garlands, confetti and various musical instruments.

In 1960, baritone Paulo Fortes wanted to protest at the 19th-century operatic composer Carlos Gomes being forgotten. Fortes raised funds to release the maquette for the statue that Rodolfo Bernardelli had made for the city of Campinas (Gomes' birthplace) from the National School of Fine Arts. He had a new statue cast in a foundry on Rua Camerino, recruited four

removal men and, in the morning, "confiscated" the Chopin statue. After lying forgotten for a while in a warehouse, the sculpture was finally restored to Praia Vermelha in 1964. In its place, in front of the Municipal Theatre, Fortes installed the statue of the greatest composer of the Americas, Carlos Gomes. It has recently been moved round the side of the theatre.

WHY WAS CHOPIN'S STATUE PLACED IN FRONT OF THE MUNICIPAL THEATRE IN 1951?

The sculpture *Mulher com ânfora* (Woman with Amphora) by Humberto Cozzo used to stand in Praça Floriano (Cinelândia) in the early 1930s. It was designed to embellish (and conceal) the small water tower built to supply the theatre during renovations. The work was coordinated by engineer Doyle Maia under the leadership of the then mayor Pedro Ernesto, administrator of the federal district between 1931 and 1936. The base of the statue features two medallions: on one side, Pedro Ernesto, who had commissioned the work to restore the theatre and, on the other, Pereira Passos, who had originally built it.

According to Brazilian historian Raimundo Magalhães Júnior, mayor Mendes de Morais wanted to remove the figure of his predecessor Ernesto from the Cinelândia district, so he replaced Cozzo's sculpture with the Chopin statue. *Mulher com ânfora* was moved to Glória, then again in front of Candelária church, where it still stands.

STAIRCASE AT THE MUSEU DE CIÊNCIAS DA TERRA

404 Avenida Pasteur
• Open Tuesday to Sunday 10am–4pm
• Admission free
• Tel: (21) 2295-7596
• E-mail: mcter@cprm.gov.br

A dramatic forgotten staircase

The Museum of Earth Sciences is the last vestige of the Exposição Nacional held in 1908 to celebrate the centenary of the opening of the ports (see following double-page spread). It has a rich collection of minerals and a few rooms dedicated to palaeontology and geology, in a quaint but charming setting. There is a particularly striking staircase leading to beautiful offices (not open to the public). The three paintings on the stairs (allegories of trade, industry and agriculture) are the work of painter Antônio Parreiras Niterói (1860–1937), who received a gold medal at the Seville World's Fair (Expo 29) in 1929.

The building, designed in 1880 by engineer Paula Freitas to house the faculty of the University of Medicine Pedro II, was left unfinished, and work only resumed on the occasion of the National Exposition of 1908. The neoclassical building, formerly the Palácio dos Estados (States Palace), was the main pavilion. It covered 7,600 m^2 and had ninety-one rooms. The building was occupied successively by the Ministry of Agriculture, the Veterinary School of Agronomy and the National Department of Mineral Production.

Other than the National Exposition, the statues in front of the former Hotel Glória are another relic of the anniversary celebrations of the opening of the ports in 1808.

THE 1908 EXPOSIÇÃO NACIONAL: FROM "PESTILENTIAL" TO "MARVELLOUS" CITY

Between 1903 and 1906, under prefect Pereira Passos (1836–1913), Rio saw extensive urbanisation schemes to modernise the city, eliminate epidemics and reduce the number of deaths caused by its generally insalubrious conditions. The ambience had been enough to earn Rio the nickname "pestilential city".

As urban renewal was changing the face of the Federal capital, a National Exposition was organised in 1908 to present this "new" city and the country's greater integration in an increasingly metropolitan and cosmopolitan world (Brazil participated in six World's Fairs between 1862 and 1904). The date was chosen to mark the centenary of the opening of Brazil's ports to friendly nations.

In his inauguration speech, President Afonso Pena (1847–1909) stated that the exhibition was intended to "make an inventory of the country", presenting its natural resources, production capacity and economic development.

The city's advanced public services were also highlighted – in particular, statistics showing that yellow fever had been eradicated the previous year and that fewer people would now die of smallpox and bubonic plague in the Federal District.

The 1908 Exposition was held between Saudade (now the site of Rio Yacht Club) and Vermelha beaches in the Urca neighbourhood from August to November. It was a hugely successful event: a million paying visitors passed through, whereas the city had only around 800,000 residents. With over thirty pavilions, it surpassed the size of the London, Sydney and Melbourne Expos. The only pavilion that still survives is the States Pavilion, which stood not far from the monumental gates. Today it is the Museum of Earth Sciences (see p. 199), a theme related to the main focus of the Exposition.

At the far end of this axis stood the Industries Pavilion, in the former military academy. The academy had been renovated using the newly invented material, reinforced concrete. It had its own light source and imposing fountains, forming what was called the *château d'eau* (French for "water tower"). The academy was demolished in 1938 to make way for the vast Praça General Tibúrcio.

Apart from its use of new materials, the Exposition facilities also served as a showcase for infrastructure solutions and urban development: a wharf was built on Saudade beach to accommodate the boats coming from the Pharoux docks (now Praça XV), a tramway was opened on Botafogo beach, and a small train carried visitors between pavilions.

ORIGIN OF THE EXPRESSION "*CIDADE MARAVILHOSA*"

It was the writer and politician Coelho Neto (1864–1934) who in 1908, inspired by the new face of the city at the time, coined the nickname that defined Rio as the "marvellous city".

URCA

MICROFONE DO CASSINO
DA URCA - 1935

INSTITUTO CULTUREL CRAVO ALBIN

2 Avenida São Sebastião, Urca
• Tel: (21) 2295-2532
• http://institutocravoalbin.com.br
• Open Monday to Friday 11am–6pm (visits on reservation only)
• Admission free
• Bus: 107, 511, 512, 513 (link with metro at Botafogo station)

Little-known musical treasures

I n the modest building at the top of Avenida São Sebastião, nobody would guess that the narrow elevator leading to the fourth floor opens onto an area of around 3,000 m² spread over three levels, with many small rooms, a terrace and an amazing garden with spectacular views over Botafogo bay below Sugarloaf Mountain.

This is the home of the little–known Cravo Albin Cultural Institute, a non-profit organisation set up in late 2001 to promote Brazilian culture and especially its music. The institute has a notable collection of 60,000 disks (LPs, 78s and compacts) and about 5,000 CDs, reference video and music programmes, sheet music and photographs.

In an atmosphere reminiscent of a family home, filled with ancestral memories, a mini-museum displays instruments and costumes of Brazilian music personalities, pictures and craft objects.

On the fourth and fifth floors, beyond the rooms reserved for the music collection, is the reproduction of a 1930s/40s radio station with the microphone used by Carmen Miranda on Radio Mayrink Veiga. You can also see (and touch) Luiz Gonzaga's accordion, Cartola's guitar and the hats of Tom Jobim and Pixinguinha. There's also a collection of radios from different eras.

From the fifth-floor terrace you can enjoy panoramic views of Praia da Urca and the iconic former casino (Cassino da Urca), now the Instituto Europeu do Design. Follow the walkway and concrete steps at the far end for a surprise: a garden with belvedere and small oval pool standing among the rocks of Morro da Urca. There, in 1962, among the profusion of plant life, the building used for the institute's cultural events and temporary exhibitions was built out of recuperated materials. The façade is a replica of the home of Bishop José Castelo Branco's mother, Ana Teodoro, who lived between 1731 and 1805 at Cinelândia in a house that is now the Biblioteca Nacional (National Library). The area in front of her house was known as Largo da Mãe do Bispo (Square of the Bishop's Mother), the name inscribed on a plaque in the garden as a tribute to this influential figure of colonial Rio.

GUIDED TOUR OF FORTE SÃO JOSÉ ⓲

Avenida João Luiz Alves
Urca
• Open Saturday and Sunday 10am–1.30pm (duration two hours)
• Tel: (21) 2543-3323 / 2586-2291
• Reservations: sitiohistorico.fsj@gmail.com

> *Birthplace of the city, unprecedented views, Art Deco gym ...*

Book by e-mail (address above) and you can visit the remarkable site of the military fort of São José, deep in the Urca neighbourhood, just beyond the famous Urca bar.

The guided tour, which lasts two hours, begins with the sports museum (where various sporting artefacts of rather limited interest are displayed) before heading to the fort itself on Morro Cara de Cao – the opportunity for a very pleasant walk of around fifteen minutes, offering superb and unusual views of the city and the two private beaches that are part of the site.

São José fort, originally built in 1565 and renovated in 1872, together with Santa Cruz fort, on the other side of Guanabara bay at Niterói (which you can see clearly during the visit), was part of the bay's defence system. An interesting historical museum completes the fort tour.

On the way back, you pass the remarkable Art Deco building that was the first covered gymnasium in Latin America. Note the delightful figures in Portuguese stone that celebrate different sports.

The tour ends at a remarkable site in every respect: the charming Praia de Fora, where Estácio de Sá berthed his ship on 1 March 1565 and founded the city. The foundation stone at the site, set back from the beach, is a copy of the original, which is in the Igreja dos Capuchinhos (Capuchin church) at Tijuca.

Some people consider, therefore, that Ladeira São Sebastião, which begins near the old Urca casino and ends at São José fort, is the oldest street in Rio.

IPANEMA - LEBLON
LAGOA - GAVEA
JARDIM BOTANICO
HUMAITA

COFFEE ROUTE

❶

Trailhead: end of Rua Sarah Villela in Jardim Botânico
- Distance and duration: 6km / 4h (well marked but difficult trail)
- Free
- Tel: (21) 2491-1700 (Parque Nacional da Tijuca)

> *Historical route to the Christ statue*

The coffee route, different from Parque Lage's widely known path, is the best way of reaching the Cristo Redentor (Christ the Redeemer). It winds through the lush vegetation of the Mata Atlântica (Atlantic forest), passing by two waterfalls, a colonial road and two watchtowers with breathtaking views. As a bonus, you're likely to come across marmosets (*Callithrix penicillata*) and other primates. But be aware that despite the excellent maintenance and signposting provided by the Tijuca Forest National Park in collaboration with volunteer groups Terra Limpa and Ecotribo, the trail is long and steep. It is advisable to set off early in the morning.

The trail starts at the end of Rua Sarah Villela. After the last house, it's another 200m or so to a small paved square, where the path begins. Although the first section is steep and signposted with yellow arrows, after about ten minutes it joins the Transcarioca trail. At this junction, turn right. From there, just follow the yellow marks painted on rocks and trees.

After another 15-minute walk, the trail crosses the Primatas river opposite the first waterfall (Cachoeira dos Primatas). Just beyond the fork in the path, it's a good idea to climb up to the left and bathe in the second Primates' waterfall before retracing your steps to rejoin the Transcarioca trail. You'll pass the beautiful Lagoa viewpoint before arriving at Vale do Rio Cabeça. This stretch is often frequented by groups of monkeys making a racket while swinging on branches and jumping from tree to tree. With a little luck you might also spot a toucan.

From Vale do Rio Cabeça the history of the trail grows richer. The fully paved route follows the contour lines. Note the remains of retaining walls, old houses and stone bridges. This road was built to transport coffee and other goods from Paneiras to Chácara do Rio Cabeça (so named because it was thought that the waters could cure migraine - *cabeça* meaning head).

According to the writings of Maria Graham in the early 19th century, Vale do Rio Cabeça hosted "extensive coffee plantations, interspersed with numerous orange, lemon and other shrubs that seem to be more a variation of the forest rather than a meeting of cultivated and wild land".

Thanks to the painstaking work of Thomás Nogueira da Gama, this region was completely reforested from 1862. A sharp eye will also be able to identify various exotic species such as jackfruit and some coffee plants.

Near Paneiras, the route passes close to a millennial fig tree, whose trunk is believed to be the largest of any on the Transcarioca trail.

Approaching the end of the path, you'll come to two forks, both well signposted. At the first one, keep right, while at the second you leave the main Transcarioca trail to turn left and follow the wooden arrows to 'Corcovado'. After crossing the railway track it's ten more minutes to the Christ statue.

There are several options for the return trip: train, bus, walking down the route and the Transcarioca trail to Lage park, although this is not recommended for inexperienced hikers.

CAPELA DE NOSSA SENHORA DA CABEÇA ❷

80 Rua Faro
Jardim Botânico
• Open Monday to Friday 9am—4pm
• Mass 12 August, feast day of Our Lady of Cabeça, and other occasions
• Tel: (21) 3091-9007

One of Rio's most delightful secrets

Not far from Rio's botanical gardens, hidden at the end of Rua Faro behind a large metal gate, the Casa Maternal Mello Mattos houses a school run by Carmelite nuns who also live there. Just ring the bell on weekdays, between 9am and 4pm, to share one of Rio's most delightful secrets: at the top of the hill stands a lovely little chapel built in 1603, one of the oldest buildings in Rio de Janeiro.

This serene chapel, whose atmosphere is conducive to prayer, will be opened for you on request.

It was built on the Engenho d'El Rey sugar plantation, which at the time extended over almost the entire area of what is now the Jardim Botânico. It was used as a private chapel by the estate owner, Governor Martim Correia, a member of whose family brought an image of Our Lady of Cabeça back from Portugal.

The story goes that St Euphrasius (1st century AD), the first bishop of the city of Andújar in southern Spain, received from the hands of St Peter a cedar statue of the Virgin, made by St Luke himself. On his return home, the bishop had a shrine built to house the statue. During the Muslim conquest of southern Spain, the local people hid this image in a cave on Monte Cabeça. It wasn't until 12 August 1227 that one Juan Alonso de Rivas, who had lost his right arm fighting the Muslims, discovered the hidden statue. The Virgin then restored his arm, a miracle that led to the rapid spread of the cult of Nossa Senhora da Cabeça (Our Lady of the Head), from the name of the hill where the statue had been found.

According to legend, the statue of Nossa Senhora da Cabeça was carved by St Luke, who lived at the time of the Virgin and probably knew her personally. It therefore possessed the immense distinction (like the crucifix of Lucca, in Tuscany, or the Holy Shroud of Turin, in the case of Jesus) of representing her *true* face. The original statue disappeared during the Spanish Civil War in 1937.

NEARBY

THE FIG TREE IN RUA FARO

At 51 Rua Faro, an imposing 300-year-old fig tree was threatened with being felled to make way for a new building. Defended by the residents' association (and its then president, Leonel Kaz), the fig tree has not only been preserved but is listed as heritage, thus becoming the first protected tree in the history of Brazil.

STATUE OF THE *ORIXÁ* OSSANHA ❸

Botanical Garden
1008 Rua Jardim Botânico
• Tel: (21) 3874-1808
• www.jbrj.gov.br
• Open Monday 12 noon–5pm, Tuesday to Sunday 8am–5pm (closes one hour later in summer)
• Admission: R$7 (free for children under 7 and the over-60s)

Rare image of an African-Brazilian deity in Rio

At the far end of Rio's Botanical Garden, near the Rua Pacheco Leão exit in a rarely visited corner, is one of Rio's most intriguing statues, where followers of African-Brazilian traditions meet regularly.

The 5-metre-tall resin sculpture of Ossanha, an African-Brazilian deity or *orixá* (orisha), was designed in 2004 by artist Tatti Moreno, born on 18 December 1944 in Salvador de Bahia. A small sign at the statue's feet evokes the mystical and healing secrets of leaves and plants.

The *orixá* Ossanha (also known, according to various traditions, as Ossanyin, Ossaim, Ossãe or Ossain), as the deity of leaves and herbs, couldn't have found a better site in Rio than here in the Botanical Garden. He is symbolised by a metal rod terminating in seven points reaching for the sky. A bird soars from the central point.

The legend goes that Ossanha had received the secret of leaves from supreme god Olodumare. Ossanha knew that some leaves brought calmness or energy; others brought luck, glory, honours, or on the other hand misery, disease and accidents. Other *orixás* held no power over plants and depended on Ossanha to stay healthy and be successful in their endeavours.

Xangô (Shango), the impatient, impetuous warrior, annoyed by this state of affairs, plotted to steal the secret of plants from Ossanha. He explained to his wife Lansã that sometimes Ossanha hung a container on an iroko branch with his most powerful leaves inside. "Brew up a powerful storm on one of these days," Xangô told her. Lansã accepted the mission with alacrity.

The wind blew in great gusts, ripping the roofs from houses, uprooting trees, destroying everything in its path, and finally unhooking the container from where it was hanging. It was carried far away and the leaves all flew out.

The *orixás* recovered them all. Each *orixá* became the owner of certain leaves, but Ossanha remained the "master of the secret" of their virtues and the words that had to be said to activate them.

ENTRANCE TO THE ACADEMIA IMPERIAL DE BELAS ARTES ❹

Jardim Botânico
1008 Rua Jardim Botânico
• Open: Monday 12 noon–5pm, Tues–Sun 8am–5pm (closes an hour later in summer)
• Admission: R$7 (free for children under 7 and the over 60s)
• Over 60s (plus one companion) can ride through the park in an electric car for free – the walk takes about forty minutes
• Bus: all lines pass through Rua Jardim Botânico
• Tel: (21) 3874-1808
• www.jbrj.gov.br

A movable feast for the eyes

In Rio's Botanical Garden, at the end of Barbosa Rodrigues avenue, lined with its immense imperial palms and bamboo, stands the imposing neoclassical entrance to the former Imperial Academy of Fine Arts. This entrance was not always here; designed in the early 19th century by French architect Auguste-Henri-Victor Grandjean de Montigny, it was moved to the gardens in 1938 when the city centre Academy was demolished to make way for the Ministry of Finance, which was eventually built elsewhere (see p. 64). Today, the former site of the Academy is a car park.

After the Portuguese court moved to Rio in 1808, major scientific expeditions visited the country. In March 1816 the Missão Artística Francesa (French Artistic Mission) sailed to Rio to teach art and architecture. The forty members of the mission, including Jean-Baptiste Debret and Grandjean de Montigny, had a strong academic background. The Academy was founded the same year but was not inaugurated until 1826 under the name Academia Imperial de Belas Artes. In the 20th century the Academy was absorbed by the Federal University of Rio de Janeiro and became known as the Escola de Belas Artes (School of Fine Arts).

MESTRE VALENTIM AT THE BOTANICAL GARDEN

In the violet nursery in the centre of the park, a memorial to Mestre Valentim preserves the remains of two of his wonderful fountains. These are the statues of Echo and Narcissus, the first cast metal sculptures in Brazil. They originally formed part of the Marrecas fountain, installed in 1785 at the junction of Rua das Belas Noites (later Rua das Marrecas because of the fountain) and what is now Rua Evaristo da Veigam towards the main entrance to the Passeio Público (Public Promenade, see p. 120). The other two works on display are sculptures of wading birds (egrets or herons), which formerly graced the Fonte dos Jacarés (Caiman fountain) on the Passeio Público, opened in 1783.

Near the Academy entrance and the *pernambuco* (brazil-wood) grove, you can see the gateway of the Real Fábrica de Pólvora (Royal Gunpowder Factory) and the Oficina do Moinho dos Pilões (Workshop of the Pressing Mill). The factory was founded in 1808 by Dom João and occupied the former headquarters of Engenho Rodrigo de Freitas sugar cane presses. The gateway and some sections of wall are all that remain. At the entrance to the workshop, known as the Casa dos Pilões (House of the Presses) where the powder was compressed, you can still see the great stone wheels that were used to grind coal and sulphur. There is a small museum and archaeological site there now.

GÁVEA ROUTE MARKERS

⑤

Opposite 10 Estrada da Gávea
• Bus: 170, 537, 538, 539

*Forgotten
route markers*

Opposite number 10 Estrada de Gávea stands one of the route markers erected in the city in the 1930s. You can still pick out the directions on both sides, "R.M.S. Vicente 01" (Rua Marques de São Vicente) and "Av. Niemeyer" (this one obscured by graffiti). The initials "PDF" (Prefecture of the Federal District), dating from the time when Rio was the capital of the Republic, are inscribed on the other side.

These markers were used to measure distances between locations: "from 1,000 in 1,000 metres", as specified by the road signage regulations of 1928.

Over time, they have lost some of the reasons for their existence and many have been withdrawn. Today, research shows that thirty-four of these "forgotten" markers are still at their original sites. Most of them are in the western suburbs of Rio (mainly at Campo Grande, Guaratiba and Sepetiba), but some can also be seen in the north and on the roads of Vista Chinesa, Joá and Paineiras in the middle of Tijuca forest. The marker on Estrada da Gávea seems to be the only one left in the city's southern zone.

The Circuit de Gávea, a motor race known around the world and held between 1933 and 1954 (with a break during the Second World War), skirted Morro Dois Irmãos. The circuit of approximately 11 km began at Rua Marques de São Vicente (the start was near what is now the Gávea shopping centre). It continued along Bartolomeu Mitre, Visconde de Albuquerque and Niemeyer avenues, as far as Estrada da Gávea, via what is now Rocinha and down to the route marker. With over a hundred bends and a variety of road surfaces (asphalt, cement, paving stones, sand), the circuit has seen many serious accidents.

A MOTOR RACE THAT INSPIRED THE RIO CARNAVAL

In 1937, Germany was represented by legendary driver Hans Stuck racing under the Nazi flag. The race was eventually won by the Italian Carlo Pintacuda, who became the "Hero of Gávea" of his day. In Carioca slang, Pintacuda means "courage" or "bold". Years later, during the 1950 Carnaval, it inspired the "March of the Stutterer" ("I'm s-soft when I s-speak / But I'm a Pintucada when I kiss").

ESOTERICISM OF THE BRAZILIAN FLAG ③

Since independence, Brazil has mainly been represented by two flags: the old flag of the Empire and the new flag of the Republic. In 1822, the Brazilian imperial flag had a green background with a central yellow diamond, within which a green coat of arms consisted of a circle containing nineteen stars (representing the states). At the centre of this circle, an armillary sphere was set on the Cross of the Order of Christ. Above the coat of arms was the crown of the Empire of Brazil. Below, two interlaced branches (coffee and tobacco plants) climbed up the sides. The green and yellow colours were chosen by Emperor Dom Pedro I in person: green for his family, the royal house of Bragança; and yellow for the Habsburg family of his first wife, Maria Leopoldina of Austria. Pedro I commissioned the design from renowned French artist Jean-Baptiste Debret (1768–1848), a Freemason who had associated himself in the meantime with Brazilian Masonry through the minister José Bonifácio de Andrada e Silva. The artist would have greatly influenced the emperor in his choice of colours, which were, indeed, those of the secret society he'd founded, the Nobre Ordem dos Cavaleiros da Santa Cruz (Noble Order of the Knights of the Holy Cross), known as the Apostalado (Apostolate), to which the ruler belonged under the title of Archon, Head of the Apostolate. It was opposed both to absolute monarchy and to a secular republic and envisaged an ideal state where the emperor would be a sage (symbolised by the colour yellow) in a kingdom of peace and creativity (symbolised by the colour green). The Apostolate was closed down on 23 June 1823.

Later, on 19 November 1889, following a proposal from Benjamin Constant, a provisional government decree approved the current national flag of Brazil, keeping the structure of the imperial flag, bearing the inscription *Ordem e Progresso* (Order and Progress) inspired by the maxim of Positivist philosopher Auguste Comte: "Love as a principle and order as the basis; progress as the goal". The yellow and green flag was designed by painter Décio Vilares. It consists of a green rectangle symbolising the Brazilian forests and in the centre a yellow diamond evoking the country's mineral wealth, especially gold. The blue starry sphere in the centre of the diamond represents the astronomical aspect of the Rio de Janeiro sky at 8.30am on 15 November 1889, the day of the Proclamation of the Republic. This sphere originally contained 21 stars (currently 27), symbolising the national states and the federal district:

Acre – Gamma Hydrae (Dhanab al Shuja); Amapá – Beta Canis Majoris (Mirzam); Amazonas – Alpha Canis Minoris (Procyon); Pará – Alpha Virginis (Spica); Maranhão – Beta Scorpii (Graffias); Piauí – Alpha Scorpii (Antares); Ceará – Epsilon Scorpii (Wei); Rio Grande do Norte – Lambda Scorpii (Shaula); Paraíba – Kappa Scorpii (Girtab); Pernambuco – Mu Scorpii (Denebokab); Alagoas – Theta Scorpii (Sargas); Sergipe – Iota Scorpii (Apollyon);

Bahia – Gamma Crucis (Gacrux); Espírito Santo – Epsilon Crucis (Intrometida); Rio de Janeiro – Beta Crucis (Mimosa); São Paulo – Alpha Crucis (Acrux); Paraná – Gamma Trianguli Australis; Santa Catarina – Beta Trianguli Australis; Rio Grande do Sul – Alpha Trianguli Australis; Minas Gerais – Delta Crucis (Pálida); Goiás – Alpha Carinae (Canopus); Mato Grosso – Alpha Canis Majoris (Sirius); Mato Grosso do Sul – Alpha Hydrae (Alphard); Rondônia – Gamma Canis Majoris (Muliphen); Roraima – Delta Canis Majoris (Wezen); Tocantins – Epsilon Canis Majoris (Adhara); Brasília (Distrito Federal) – Sigma Octantis (Polaris Australis).

These stars on the flag are not just for decorative effect, but have a real esoteric meaning. According to the Egyptian Hermetic tradition, rediscovered in Europe in the Renaissance (see *Secret Florence* in this series of guides), which was well known to Brazilian Freemasons and Positivists: "That which is below is like that which is above and that which is above is like that which is below." This correspondence between the macrocosm and the microcosm means that the representation of the sky at a given date on the ceiling of a room (as in some palaces and churches in Rome, and Florence in particular) or a flag, as here, is expected to attract celestial energy in the place of representation. Representing it on a flag to be flown throughout the country was meant, in the minds of its creators, to attract celestial energies to the entire Brazilian territory.

Critics, however, say that the arrangement of stars is the reverse of the constellations visible in the Southern Hemisphere. The flag is, in fact, a mirror that reflects the night sky, hence the reversal of positions and astral correlation. Don't forget that Emperor Dom Pedro II, as well as astronomers Luís Cruls and Manuel Pereira Reis, and of course Décio Vilares himself, were keen astrologers and they placed the stars on the flag with the constitutional support of the Brazilian Masonic Order in which the Republican Club of Master Mason Lopes Trovão played a leading role.

1. PARÁ
   Spica (α Virginis)
2. AMAZONAS
   Prócion (α Canis Minoris)
3. MATO GROSSO DO SUL
   Alphard (α Hydrae)
4. RONDÔNIA
   Wezen (δ Canis Majoris)
5. MATO GROSSO
   Sírio (α Canis Majoris)
6. RORAIMA
   Muliphen (γ Canis Majoris)
7. AMAPÁ
   Mirzam (β Canis Majoris)
8. TOCANTINS
   Adhara (ε Canis Majoris)
9. GOIÁS
   Canopus (α Carinae)
10. BAHIA
    Gacrux (γ Crucis)
11. MINAS GERAIS
    Pálida (δ Crucis)
12. ESPÍRITO SANTO
    Intrometida (ε Crucis)
13. SÃO PAULO
    Acrux (α Crucis)
14. ACRE
    Dhanab al Shuja (γ Hydrae)
15. PIAUÍ
    Antares (α Scorpii)
16. MARANHÃO
    Graffias (β Scorpii)
17. CEARÁ
    Wei (ε Scorpii)
18. RIO GRANDE DO NORTE
    Shaula (λ Scorpii)
19. PARAÍBA
    Girtab (κ Scorpii)
20. PERNAMBUCO
    Denebakrab (μ Scorpii)
21. ALAGOAS
    Sargas (θ Scorpii)
22. SERGIPE
    Apollyon (ι Scorpii)
23. SANTA CATARINA
    δ Trianguli Australis
24. RIO GRANDE DO SUL
    Atria (α Trianguli Australis)
25. PARANÁ
    γ Trianguli Australis
26. RIO DE JANEIRO
    Mimosa (β Crucis)
27. BRASÍLIA
    Polaris Australis (σ Octantis)

OCCULT SIGNIFICANCE OF MORRO DOIS IRMÃOS

Long before Ipanema acquired its present characteristics, Morro Dois Irmãos (Two Brothers hill) had already caught the attention of the Tupinambás, members of the Tupí tribe who lived on the coast. They devoted a special cult to the rock, described in Capuchin chronicles along with the local legends associated with it. Even the name Ipanema, "unclean water" (not fit to drink, referring to the salt water of the nearby ocean), is Tupí in origin.

Tupí religious culture was based on nature worship, in which stone shapes were very important. Such was the case of this peak, whose cone is superimposed on another triangular shape. The pair were associated very early on with Jacy (Moon, Woman) and Tupan (Sun, Man), in other words the Earth's two main stars that punctuate day and night, the activity of the body and the repose of the soul. They were nicknamed the *irmãos* (siblings).

The celebration of this stone cult was practised by the indigenous people in the following way: in the highlands, they worshipped the Sun (Tupan) with dances and war chants evoking the solar force, where men dominated; and in the lowlands, they worshipped the Moon (Jacy) with dances and songs evoking maternal energy, represented by the waters of the ocean and led by women. As they needed a totemic symbol of the two celestial bodies, the rocky mound of Upabanem (Ipanema) with its suggestive contours was chosen.

But the story doesn't stop there: in the 16th century, the present region of Rio de Janeiro and Niteroi was occupied by the Tupinambá tribe of the Termiminós, whose chief was the famous Arariboia. Born around 1523, he helped the Portuguese to expel the French and their Tamoios allies from the region by his decisive victory at the battle of Uruçu-mirim (now Flamengo beach) on 20 January 1567. In return for his support, Arariboia received from the King of Portugal, Dom Sebastião, the cross and coat of a Knight of the Order of Christ. He was also given a woman of mixed Portuguese and Brazilian blood, with whom he had a large number of offspring who later interbred with the family of Antonio de Mariz Coutinho (Barcelos, 1537–Brazil, 1584). Arariboia converted to Christianity and took the name Martim Afonso de Souza, in homage to the Portuguese navigator. He died in 1574. In order to perpetuate the memory of heroic Arariboia and his wife, who had contributed so much to the Brazilian people, shortly after his death the Termiminós decided that Morro Dois Irmãos represented their great leader and his wife, incarnations of Tupan and Jacy, the supreme deities of the Tupí pantheon.

Some even go further back in time to claim that the name "Morro Dois Irmãos", which dominates Pedra da Gávea, evokes the memory of "Phoenician Brazil". In 1000 BC Baal-Zir, the exiled King of Tyre, capital of Phoenicia, is thought to have arrived here with his court and family, including his twin children, the boy Yet-Baal-Bey and the girl Yet-Baal-Bel. The memory of these two would be perpetuated in the name Morro Dois Irmãos, which along with Pedra da Gávea formed a triad of stones symbolising the Sun, Moon and Earth. Legend or not, the fact is that the

Phoenicians were the greatest navigators of early history and reached the most distant lands of the Western Sea (the Atlantic) according to several historians. And in their religion, these three celestial bodies played a decisive role, especially the Sun called Baal (Lord), the same meaning that the Tupí gave to Tupan.

A magical memory of Rio de Janeiro's forgotten past, Morro Dois Irmãos is still there, shrouded by mysterious mists, effacing time. Even São Paulo singer Chico Buarque admits: *Dois Irmãos, quando vai alta a madrugada / E a teus pés vão-se encostar os instrumentos / Aprenti a respeitar tua prumada / E desconfiar do teu silêncio* (Two Brothers off to the heights at dawn / And your feet facing the instruments / I learned to respect your peaks / And be wary of your silence).

BUGLE BOY STATUE ⑧

Corner of Rua Visconde de Pirajá and Rua Garcia D'Ávila
Ipanema
• Metro: Nossa Senhora da Paz

**Memories
of Bahia
in Ipanema**

At the corner of Visconde de Pirajá and Garcia D'Ávila streets, near the electricity pole, is a curious bronze statue of a soldier blowing a bugle, his foot resting on a cannon half-buried in the sidewalk. This caricature is in tribute to Corporal Luís Lopes, bugler to the Brazilian forces fighting for independence in the province of Bahia, 1822–1823.

Unveiled in 2004, the unusual style of the statue caused some controversy. Even the story of Corporal Luis and his role in the battle of Pirajá of 8 November 1822 is controversial. The battle wasn't going well for the Brazilians, who were outnumbered by the Portuguese. Their commander Major José de Barros Falcão, sensing imminent defeat, ordered the bugler to sound the retreat. The corporal disobeyed orders and instead sounded the 'cavalry, advance and behead'. Luís Lopes surprised and panicked the Portuguese, who dispersed,

giving the advantage to the Brazilian troops.

In the absence of official documents, some claim that this incident never happened. But the poem *Paraguaçu* by Ladislau Titaro, an eyewitness to the battle of Pirajá, mentions the feat of Luís Lopes. There is no doubt that the Brazilians won this battle, finally defeating the Portuguese on 2 July 1823, ten months after Dom Pedro I had declared independence on the banks of the Ipiranga river in São Paulo on 7 September 1822.

ANOTHER IPANEMA TRIBUTE TO BAHIA'S INDEPENDENCE HEROES

When the neighbourhood was urbanised after the founding of Vila Ipanema in 1884, many streets paid tribute to family members and friends of the entrepreneurs José Antonio Moreira Filho, Baron of Ipanema, and Antonio José da Silva. In 1922, during the independence centenary celebrations, the names of some streets were changed to honour the heroes who had fought in the War of Independence. Rua Otávio Silva, for example, became Rua Maria Quitéria, and Rua 20 Novembro, which commemorated the birthday of the baron's wife, was changed to Rua Visconde de Pirajá.

Maria Quitéria (1792–1853) is the 'woman soldier of Brazil'. When she learned of the struggle for independence, she ran away from home, cut off her long hair, disguised herself as a man and enlisted as a volunteer in the armed forces of Bahia.

Joana Angélica (1761–1822), martyr, succumbed to the blows of Portuguese soldiers' bayonets in attempting to defend the convent of Lapa, in Salvador, where she was mother superior.

Visconde de Pirajá: perhaps the most important leader of the movement was Joaquim Pires de Carvalho e Albuquerque (1788–1848), a wealthy landowner known as 'Colonel Santinho'. He received the title of Viscount (Visconde) of Pirajá after his victory on home soil.

Barão de Jaguaripe: Francisco Elesbão Pires de Carvalho e Albuquerque (1787–1856) consolidated the independence of Bahia and was proclaimed president of the revolutionary junta that governed the province. He was the Viscount of Pirajá's brother.

Barão da Torre: Antonio Joaquim Pires de Carvalho e Albuquerque (1774–1852), whose full title was Barão da Torre (Baron of the Tower) of Garcia D'Ávila, turned his castle into an operational base for the independence forces. Another brother of the Visconde de Pirajá, he also became his son-in-law when he married one of the viscount's daughters.

The Pirajá district of the municipality of Salvador, where the battle of that name was fought on 8 November 1822 (see opposite), is a word of Tupí origin. It means 'full of fish' through the juxtaposition of *pirá* (fish) and *îá* (filled).

H. STERN WORLD HEADQUARTERS MUSEUM ❾

113 Rua Garcia D'Ávila
Ipanema
• Open Monday to Friday 9am—6pm, Saturday 9am—12 noon
• www.hstern.net

The world's largest collection of tourmalines

If the tour of jeweller H. Stern's workshops is relatively well known (a must for anyone who hasn't yet tried it), the private museum, with its extraordinary collection of tourmalines, is much less frequented: many visitors to the workshops don't even know it exists.

And for good reason: it's hidden behind a heavy door, kept closed, and you have to specifically ask to visit.

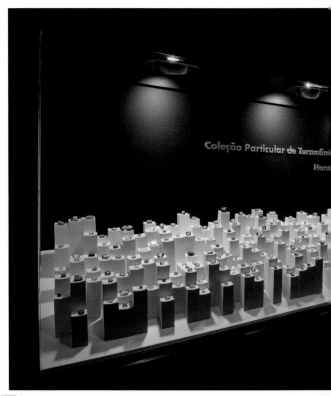

The museum itself is an absolute treasure trove. The highlight is Hans Stern's private collection of 1,007 tourmalines in all the colours, shapes and sizes imaginable – the largest in the world.

On his arrival in Brazil in 1939, Stern (1922–2007) started work as a commercial typist. Six years later, in 1945, he had already founded the company H. Stern Jewelers, which now has around 3,000 employees.

Throughout his career, Stern sought to awaken and whet the public's appetite for coloured gemstones (aquamarines, tourmalines, amethysts and topaz, among others) in a market that formerly only valued diamonds, rubies, sapphires and emeralds.

Ironically, he was born partially sighted and only gained some vision in his right eye at the age of 2.

TRIOMPHE DE GALATÉE VASE BY FRANÇOIS GIRARDON ⑩

Praça José de Acioli
Ipanema

> An
> exceptional
> copy
> of a vase
> in the Louvre

Despite what some might think, Rio is not just breathtaking landscapes, although some of its artworks are almost overwhelmed by the beauty of their surroundings. If proof were needed, on the shores of Lagoa Rodrigo de Freitas in Ipanema is a round plaza with stunning views of the lagoon, Corcovado in the background and Cristo Redentor on the heights. An unusual marble vase with a strange history has stood in this little plaza for over sixty years, covered with a thick layer of plaster.

Recently the prefecture decided to give the vase a facelift and discovered that the plaster actually concealed a very fine piece of artistically carved Carrara marble, on which they had no information. When was it made and by whom? How did it arrive here? And why was it plastered over?

An Ipanema resident eventually came across the original vase at the Louvre in Paris. The *Triomphe de Galatée* (Galatea Triumphant) was one of a pair commissioned by Louis XIV in 1683 for the gardens of Versailles. After two hundred years in the royal gardens the vase was transferred to Saint-Cloud near Paris, where it stood for several years until the Louvre gave it a home in 1872. It can still be seen there today.

A few copies of this vase have turned up in major art collections around the world, including the Wallace Collection in London. Some have been offered for sale in international auctions. They are usually made from cheaper materials, such as earthenware or bronze. The only known marble copy is this one in Ipanema. It is of exceptional quality and most likely dates from the 19th century.

MUSEU DE FAVELA (MUF)

7 Rua Nossa Senhora de Fátima
Morro do Cantagalo, Ipanema
• Daily tours Monday to Friday 9am–5pm, with local guides (in Portuguese, sometimes with English, French, German or Spanish translations)
• R$60 (for Brazilians) to R$100 (other nationalities)
• Solo tours also offered
• Metro: General Osório / Ipanema
• Reservation by phone: (21) 2267-6374
• www.museudefavela.org

> **2,050 steps in a favela history lesson**

The Favela Museum, set up in 2008, tells the story of the communities of Pavão-Pavãozinho and Cantagalo through graffiti painted on three gateways and on the façades of about twenty houses in the *favela*.

Museum staff – all *favela* residents – explain that the tour itinerary corresponds to 2,050 steps along the neighbourhood's winding, narrow alleys. This is a three-hour walk through the heart of the *favela*.

As well as this tour, the museum runs a wide range of activities: gastronomy, dance classes, capoeira and graffiti, even workshops to teach you to build and fly a kite. According to social museology concepts, the MUF is Brazil's first territorial museum: the whole neighbourhood and its assets, both tangible and intangible, form part of the "collection". It's a living museum, transformed every day.

Its headquarters is in a historic building: the first brick building in the *favela* that hasn't been demolished. In the 1950s, brick buildings were prohibited in Rio but, in 1978, the small chapel of Nossa Senhora da Fátima (Our Lady of Fatima) in Cantagalo resisted and other brick buildings have gradually emerged. This type of housing was only allowed on the city's hills in the early 1980s.

From here the MUF promotes other activities, such as travelling exhibitions to preserve the memory of the *favela* and to raise the self-esteem and identity of its people, as well as selling local crafts. The terrace has a fine view of the architecture of this *favela* of some 20,000 people, with a very special backdrop: the ocean at Ipanema, Rodrigo Freitas lagoon, Corcovado and Morro Dois Irmãos.

The graffiti, signed by twenty-five artists and coordinated by one of them (all born and raised in Cantagalo), retrace the conditions and highlights of the *favela*'s history and daily life: the first water supply; migrants from the Northeast; life at a time when there was no electricity, no running water and no sanitation; religion; leisure and culture in the community, etc. As the graffiti were not all made or restored at the same time, their state of conservation varies. Part of the admission fee for the visit goes to preserving the graffiti as well as helping locals and guides, all trained in partnership with city universities.

The *favela* has benefited from the services of a Unidade de Polícia Pacificadora (Police Pacification Unit) since December 2009.

PARQUE NATURAL MUNICIPAL DA CATACUMBA TO HUMAITÁ TRAIL

Lagoa
• Tel: (21) 2247-9949
• Free

Effort in / beauty out

The stretch of the Transcarioca trail from Catacumba park to Humaitá shows the clearest link between "effort in" and "beauty out" of all Rio's landscapes. Taking advantage of the steps and the ruins of the Catacumba *favela* – razed in 1970 to make way for a sculpture park (decorated with striking work by, among others, Carybé, Frans Krajcberg and Bruno Giorgi) – the trail was opened in 1997.

The layout, which is well marked and maintained, runs by the sculptures before entering the forest, the result of successful reforestation and proof that it's possible to recuperate run-down areas. The ascent is by the steep stone paths of the former *favela*, with some stopping points where information

boards tell the story of the *favela*, reforestation and wildlife, such as silvery marmosets and toucans.

After half an hour's walk you arrive at Sacopã belvedere, which rises to 134 m and offers one of the best views of Rio, taking in Pedra da Gávea, Morro Dois Irmãos, Ipanema beach, Christ the Redeemer, the Botanical Garden and Rodrigo de Freitas lagoon. From here the trail continues to Urubu belvedere, where in addition to the spectacular view, you can also abseil (Lagoa Aventuras (21) 4105-0079 / 7870-9162).

Next, the path descends a flight of steps from the former *favela* before branching out in two directions: to the right, you'll reach Catacumba park by the same path; to the left, the hike (much less known) continues for an hour on the Transcarioca path towards the community of Cabritos, on the highest point of Rua Vitória Régia at Humaitá. This second section has recently been taken over by the maintenance team from Catacumba park. It runs along the rock via wooden stairways and *vias ferratas* ("iron ways"). Although a guide isn't essential you need some experience and to be in good physical condition. Along this route, you can see more views of Rodrigo de Freitas lagoon and tropical plants such as bromeliads and cacti clinging to the bare rock.

CENTRO NYINGMA DE BUDISMO TIBETANO

297 Rua Casuarina
Fonte da Saudade
• Open to the public for meditation on Sunday mornings 9am–10am,
Mondays at 8pm, Tuesdays at 7pm, Thursdays at 8:45pm; recitation of
mantras Sundays 10am–11am; other occasional open days – check with
the centre's website
• Tel: (21) 2527-9388
• instituto@nyingmario.org.br
• www.nyingmario.org.br

A voyage back in time

Hidden in the foothills of Morro da Saudade, the Nyingma Tibetan Buddhism Centre is one of the best-kept secrets of Lagoa. From Rua Fonte da Saudade, follow Rua Bogari until you reach Rua Casuarina. Just past the barrier, a wooden door on the left guards the entrance to the temple.

The entrance is the most spectacular part of the centre; deep within the small courtyard, a stupa (Buddhist traditional monument housing sacred relics) welcomes visitors against a background of the Corcovado statue of Christ - a lovely symbol of communion between religions.

The lie of the land gives you a real feeling of immersion in almost virgin nature, despite the tops of two buildings glimpsed down below. Framed by the centre and its prayer flags, the spectacle of stupa, forest, rock and Christ is an invitation to meditate for a moment on the benches provided.

The centre welcomes visitors several times a week for meditation sessions or mantra recitations. During our visit, the mantras left us with a deep sense of well-being.

WHERE DOES THE NAME FONTE DA SAUDADE COME FROM?

The Fonte da Saudade (Fountain of Sorrow) neighbourhood takes its name from a fountain that really did exist. Until the early 19th century, women came to do their laundry there, a few steps from what used to be Piaçava beach. It was also from here, before Rua Jardim Botânico had been constructed, that Prince Regent Dom João took the boat to the Botanical Garden on his way from Botafogo.

The water of the fountain had legendary magical properties; anyone drinking it could never forget the beauty of the place. The fountain was demolished when land was reclaimed from the lagoon during works carried out under Mayor Carlos Sampaio (1920–1922). A reproduction has since been installed at number 111 Rua Fonte da Saudade.

PARQUE DO MARTELO

41 Rua Miguel Pereira
Humaitá
• Open: Mon-Fri 8am–12 noon and 1pm–4pm, Sat-Sun 9am–1pm
• Free entry - No pets
• Tel: (21) 2527-0177

Hidden treasure of Humaitá

Strolling along the charming Rua Miguel Pereira with its many houses and small buildings, you could easily pass the wooden gate at number 41 without realising this is the entrance to a little-known urban treasure trove: Martelo park, with its gardens, fruit trees, shrubs, children's playground and physical exercise space.

The 16,000m² park on the slopes of Morro do Martelo, situated within a residential area, is the result of the local people's long struggle to block a 200-apartment development. In the successful conclusion to this 'war' the prefecture ceded the site to the residents' association of upper Hamaitá, provided they took over the maintenance of the site. The park opened in May 2005.

Once you're through the gate and access ramp, the atmosphere is one of near perfect tranquility, rare in Rio. There's a feeling of intimacy, as if you were in the garden of your own house. Indeed, there is a natural division between the children's playground and sports facilities and the rampant foliage climbing up the hill. Those who venture to the top can enjoy a panorama of the Lagoa neighbourhood and the ocean beyond Ipanema. The park, used mainly by locals, also offers a splendid view of Cristo Redentor (Christ the Redeemer) just above.

Next to the playground and outdoor shower is the administrative building where events are organised. The upkeep of the park depends on contributions from local residents and fundraising activities.

Before this zone was turned into a park, for half of the 20th century it was a small *favela*. Later it was the site of a workshop and engineering company.

As well as local residents, the battle for the park was supported by personalities such as landscaper Burle Marx, architect Oscar Niemeyer and poets Ferreira Gullar and Carlos Drummond de Andrade, who were among the signatories of a document on 15 September 1984 declaring that *"the residents' cause ... means for the city, for the community and for the neighbourhood, the preservation of a zone that constitutes ... a landscape and cultural heritage"*.

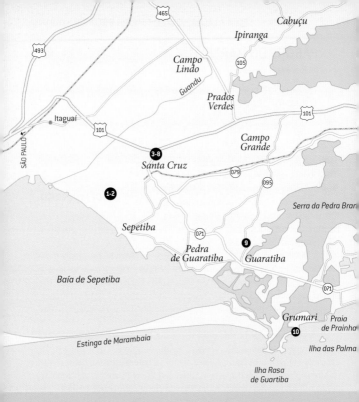

JOATINGA
SÃO CONRADO
BARRA DA TIJUCA
ZONA OESTE

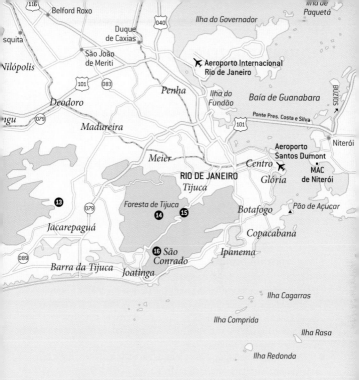

HANGAR DO ZEPPELIN

Santa Cruz Air Force Base
Rua do Império
• Train: Santa Cruz
• Bus (BRT): Santa Cruz
• From either of the adjacent stations, take bus 849
• Visits on reservation, call (21) 3078-0389 (authorisation takes around four weeks)
• Admission free

> *The world's only operational airship hangar*

The Zeppelin Hangar, the only one in the world today built for large-dimension airships, is indisputably the historical footnote to Santa Cruz Air Force Base.

Visitors to the base will find the hangar 800 m from the gate, together with a small aluminium reproduction of the zeppelin. Despite the military housing and other buildings, the tour provokes strong emotions. This vast space, set against the distant Serra do Mar mountain range, is battered by relentless winds and subjected to the rhythm of fighter jets landing and taking off, as the runway is next to the imposing hangar.

The Art Deco building, 270 m long, 50 m wide and 60 m high, is listed as a national heritage site. Originally known as Bartolomeu de Gusmão Airport – in tribute to the Portuguese priest (born in Brazil) who researched ballooning in the early 18th century – it was built to accommodate the huge German airships *Graf Zeppelin* and *Hindenburg* that serviced the Frankfurt–Rio route. Opened on 26 December 1936, the hangar stopped receiving zeppelins as a consequence of the *Hindenburg* fire in May 1937 at New Jersey.

So the gigantic hangar was only used for nine trips: four by the *LZ 129 Hindenburg* and five by the *LZ 127 Zeppelin*.

A hydrogen plant had also been built to power the airships, as well as a railway line connecting the hangar to Central do Brasil station. After the end of airship operations and the outbreak of the Second World War in 1939, the Brazilian government took over the site, which in 1942 became the Santa Cruz Air Force Base. Part of the hangar is still used for fighter aircraft maintenance.

80-TONNE DOORS

The electrical connections in the hangar have a special coating to prevent sparks that could ignite an airship. The roof is still the original, despite being exposed to very challenging climatic conditions. The smallest door, used for ventilation, was intended for moving the landing stage around. The airships entered and exited through the main doorway, whose doors weigh 80 tonnes each and take six minutes to open to 60 degrees. The control tower, on the top of the hangar, offers a view from the port of Sepetiba to the Guandu river.

TWO AIRSHIPS AND A BICYCLE

A visit to the hangar begins with the "historical room", small but very informative, offering photos and details of the airships: each had forty-five crew members and could comfortably carry thirty-five (*Graf Zeppelin*) or fifty (*Hindenburg*) passengers. There were 200 workers, nicknamed "spiders", dispersed over the runway to help move the airships around.

Also on display is an unusual bicycle, a tribute to Seu Mouzinho, who helped to build the hangar. With his experience in the general workings of the base, he was employed there until his death in 1998 and went everywhere on this bicycle. His house is now a small museum displaying the personal effects of someone who had an intimate knowledge of the history of the hangar, airships and the military base.

"SENTA A PUA" MEMORIAL

Santa Cruz Air Force Base
Rua do Império
Santa Cruz
• Train: Santa Cruz • Bus (BRT): Santa Cruz
• Arriving at either station (they are close together), take bus 849 (from the air base gateway to the monument, around 800 m)
• Visits by appointment, phone (21) 3078-0389 (authorisation can take up to four weeks)
• Admission free

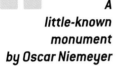

A little-known monument by Oscar Niemeyer

On the Air Force base – the home of Brazilian fighter planes and site of the spectacular Zeppelin Hangar (see p. 238) – a little-known memorial pays tribute to Brazilian airmen who fought in the Second World War. This is a forgotten project designed by architect Oscar Niemeyer.

Niemeyer's reinforced concrete conception, painted white to emphasise the spaces and increase the contrast between light and shadow, recalls the trajectory and impact of the bombs dropped by P-47 Thunderbolt aircraft of the 1st Fighter Group of the "Senta a Pua" squadron.

The inner part of the memorial lists the names of all the pilots in the squadron and houses the mausoleum of its first commander, Brigadier Nero Moura.

On the outside, the symbol "Senta a Pua" stands out, with an explanation of its meaning.

Alongside the memorial, you'll discover something rarely seen on a finished work: Niemeyer's drawings and original texts explaining his concept.

The P-47 flown by Lieutenant Lima Mendes, who completed ninety-four missions during the war, forms part of the monument.

"Senta a Pua" is the witty logo created by Flight Captain Fortunato Câmara de Oliveira, when the group was still training in the United States before leaving for Italy. The choice of an emblem sparked many discussions among the pilots. Fortunato suggested "Avestruz Voadora" ("Flying Ostrich"), a choice they all agreed with. The ostrich certainly isn't a flying creature, but its speed and agility represented the Brazilian pilot in action. Moreover, it can stomach any type of food, including American! That at least is what the pilots jokingly said; they did indeed find the GI rations very strange, although they got used to them. The ostrich is a caricature of one of these men, Lieutenant Lima Mendes. The motto comes from "Senta a Pua, Zé Maria" (literally, "You'll feel my club [hit you hard], Zé Maria"), a very popular saying in the 1940s, especially in Northeast Brazil. It was also used by pilots who, on their way to the air base, shouted to the driver: "Senta a Pua, Zé Maria!"

The memorial was unveiled on 22 April 2001, Fighter Planes Day. This commemoration has been held on that date since 1945, when in the skies over Italy the 1st Fighter Group clocked up the greatest number of missions in a single day.

PONTE DOS JESUÍTAS ❸

Estrada do Curtume,
Santa Cruz
• Train: Santa Cruz
• Bus (BRT): Santa Cruz
• From either of the adjacent stations, take bus 807

> ### *The third monument to be listed as part of the country's historic heritage*

On a bend on the road to Curtume, comfortably installed among lush pastures, a stone bridge is an unexpected sight as there is no longer a river. Originally known as the Guandu river bridge, and then the Pedro I bridge, the Bridge of the Jesuits is one of the finest examples of 18th-century Rio de Janeiro architecture. It was built in 1752 on the land of Fazenda de Santa Cruz, the Jesuit agricultural estate, as a means of crossing the Guandu river and regulating its flow by diverting the water to the Itaguaí river when necessary.

As well as protecting crops and herds, this bridge/dam mitigated the risk of flood damage to housing. Changing the course of the Guandu river – today, the main source of the city's water supply – means that the bridge has lost its purpose but it remains an important architectural monument.

During its construction, two Jesuits went to Holland to study methods of controlling water flow. The 50-metre-long and 6-metre-wide bridge was built from stone, with lime from oyster shells and fine sand. The columns, with their integrated guardrails, have Portuguese cone-shaped capitals. The base of the bridge, also stone, has four arches that allowed the volume of water to be controlled.

In the centre of the bridge stands the seal of the Society of Jesus with the Latin insignia IHS (Jesus Saviour of Men). Another Latin inscription above, engraved in the stone, warns visitors: "Kneel down before such a great name, traveller. Here also is bowed the river in spate."

In its time, the Bridge of the Jesuits (restored in 2008) was a benchmark of hydraulic engineering on a massive scale. It is the third monument to be listed as part of the nation's historic heritage.

WALLACE FOUNTAIN ❹

Praça Dom Romualdo
Santa Cruz
• Train: Santa Cruz
• Bus (BRT): Santa Cruz
• From either of the adjacent stations, take bus 872A

*A Parisian
fountain
in Santa Cruz*

During the second half of the 19th century, the English philanthropist Richard Wallace (1818–1890) offered Paris and other cities a hundred water fountains, which came to be known as "Wallace fountains". Rio de Janeiro received three of them.

The fountain in Praça Dom Romualdo at Santa Cruz originally stood in front of the former Paço Imperial of Santa Cruz (see p. 246), today Battalion Villagran Cabrita. The other two are currently in Parque da Cidade at Gávea and in the Manacás garden, Tijuca forest.

Built by the famous artistic metalworks at Val d'Osne, France, these cast-

iron fountains were designed by Charles Lebourg (1829–1906). They are decorated with statues of four draped female figures, symbolising the virtues of kindness, charity, sobriety and simplicity. On the base of each fountain is the signature of its creator: Ch. Lebourg SC 1872 – Val d'Osne.

Although the water supply doesn't seem to work any longer, the fountain in Praça Dom Romualdo has been in good condition since it was renovated in 2012.

Given the shape and vast size of the Igreja Matriz (mother church) de Nossa Senhora da Conceição near the fountain, some residents jokingly claim that its architecture reminds them of the Zeppelin Hangar (see p. 238), also in Santa Cruz. It is, in fact, inspired by the beautiful Igreja de São Francisco de Assis (Church of Saint Francis of Assisi, known as Igreja da Pampulha, Belo Horizonte, 1943), an iconic project by modernist architect Oscar Niemeyer, without having the same aesthetic qualities.

1ST BATALHÃO DE ENGENHARIA DE COMBATE ❺

35 Praça Ruão
Santa Cruz
• Train: Santa Cruz
• Bus (BRT): Santa Cruz
• From either of the adjacent stations, take right side of crossing over railway track and continue on foot to Praça Ruão
• Visits on reservation, call (21) 3395-0573
• Admission free

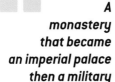

A monastery that became an imperial palace then a military academy

The former Paço Imperial (Imperial Palace) in Praça Ruão, Santa Cruz, has an impeccably preserved façade, even if interior bears little trace of its origins.

Today the headquarters of the 1st Battalion School of Military Engineering, known as Battalion Villagran Cabrita, the building's obscure history began in the 16th century when the land fell into the hands of the Jesuits. They founded the agricultural estate of Fazenda de Santa Cruz and by 1751 (the date is still visible on the main gate) a chapel and monastery had been constructed. In 1759, with the expulsion of the Jesuits from Portuguese territories, the property was returned to the Portuguese Crown. After the arrival of the royal family in Rio in 1808, the monastery was renovated to become in 1811 the Paço Real (Royal Palace) of Santa Cruz. It was designed for the greater comfort of Dom João, who remained there for months, holding public audiences and even organising receptions.

After Brazil declared independence from Portugal in 1822, the site became known as the Paço Imperial (Imperial Palace). Another floor was then added to the building. Dom Pedro II, owner of two telephones presented to him by Alexander Graham Bell, installed South America's first phone line, which connected the royal palaces of São Cristóvão and Santa Cruz. Brazil's first post office was also built in Santa Cruz in 1843 on the Rua do Comércio, now Rua Senador Camará. The imperial slaughterhouse (see p. 248), meanwhile, was opened in 1881.

During the 19th century, renowned artists such as the Frenchman Jean-Baptiste Debret, the Austrian Thomas Ender and the Englishwoman Maria Graham were welcome visitors to the palace. Reproductions of their paintings still hang in the "Green Room". There is also a small picture showing changes to the building, including the addition of the third floor, carried out during the Republican period when the property was nationalised.

After Brazil's proclamation of independence on the banks of the Ipiranga river in São Paulo, Dom Pedro I commemorated the occasion at Santa Cruz palace with members of his court, before returning to São Cristóvão.

THE CROSS THAT GAVE ITS NAME TO A NEIGHBOURHOOD

On the lawn in front of the palace stands a wooden cross, a reproduction of the one installed by the Jesuits that gave its name to the neighbourhood. There is also a stone route marker, one of twelve along the Estrada Real (Royal Road) of Santa Cruz (Holy Cross) that connected the region to the city (see p. 251).

AGRICULTURAL ESTATE OF SANTA CRUZ

The Fazenda de Santa Cruz, a Jesuit property dating from 1589, used thousands of slaves. In its heyday, there were twenty-two enclosures for various types of livestock and a wide range of plantations. The property had over twenty-five workshops with the most up-to-date facilities to meet every need, as well as a hospital, schools and even an orchestra and choir, in which the slaves played and sang. The country's first conservatoire of music was founded here.

FROM PIRACEMA TO SANTA CRUZ

The region we know today as Santa Cruz was originally populated by native peoples who called it Piracema ("place with many fish"). In 1567 the Portuguese Crown offered the region to Cristovão Monteiro, in recognition of his part in expelling the French from Guanabara bay. He set up a sugar mill and chapel at a place called Curral Falso – a name adopted by a BRT (Bus Rapid Transit) station more than four centuries later. After the death of the owner in 1589, his widow ceded the land to the Jesuits, who soon established a huge agricultural estate that they named Santa Cruz (see above).

Over the years, the whole region adopted the name Santa Cruz. Today this is the furthest suburb from Rio city centre and the third most populous. It's also a little-known gem in the country's history, especially from the 16th century to the proclamation of the republic in 1889.

RUINS OF THE IMPERIAL SLAUGHTERHOUSE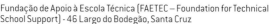

Fundação de Apoio à Escola Técnica (FAETEC – Foundation for Technical
School Support) - 46 Largo do Bodegão, Santa Cruz
• Open Monday to Friday 8am–4pm
• Visits on reservation, call (21) 2333-7228 • Admission free
• Train: Santa Cruz
• Bus (BRT): Santa Cruz, then 20-minute walk or any bus line to Sepetiba

The slaughterhouse that was once the most modern in the world

At its inauguration by Dom Pedro II in 1881, the Santa Cruz slaughterhouse in Praça Bodegão was considered to be the most modern in the world. The Palacete do Matadouro (slaughterhouse palace) and the Vila Operária (workers' village) were built alongside. While the palace is today a vibrant cultural centre, only the ruins of the slaughterhouse remain and the workers' housing has lost all its character.

The ruins of the "slaughter route" and slaughterhouse are overgrown by trees and undergrowth, but can still be visited. They give an idea of how the processing plant operated, thanks to guided tours offered by FAETEC. The *salga* (salting) room where the meat was cured is still there and now serves as the Technical School's martial arts facility. The slaughterhouse not only processed cattle, which came from neighbouring states and even Argentina (known as "gringo cattle"), but other animals such as pigs and poultry.

In the garden, the large slaughterhouse generator can still be seen. It also produced energy for lighting the surrounding streets, making Santa Cruz the

first suburb to benefit from electricity. The site had its own railway station for the transport of fresh meat. Today the abandoned station has been taken over by homeless people, but, together with the rest of the slaughterhouse buildings, it has been listed as a heritage site by the municipality.

ST GEORGE AND THE SLAUGHTERHOUSE

São Jorge is the city's most popular saint. On his feast day, 23 April, one of the biggest processions is in Praça Bodegão. For this occasion, the faithful throng the local streets on horseback, by horse and cart, or on foot. The procession has its origins in the stockbreeders from Minas Gerais who used to drive their cattle to the slaughterhouse.

The imperial slaughterhouse replaced the 1853 building at São Cristóvão, close to what is now Praça da Bandeira. But the city's first slaughterhouse, now demolished, had been built on the beach at Santa Luzia in 1774. FAETEC is located in what used to be an industrial slaughterhouse that took over in the 20th century.

PALACETE PRINCESA ISABEL ❼

Centro Cultural Municipal de Santa Cruz
Núcleo de Orintação e Pesquisa Histórica (NOPH) / Ecomuseu Santa Cruz
Rua das Palmeiras Imperiais
- www.quarteirao.com.br
- Open Monday to Friday 9am–5pm
- Visits on reservation, call (21) 99618-0672 • Admission free
- Train: Santa Cruz
- Bus (BRT): Santa Cruz

> **Home of
> the slaughterhouse
> director**

The administration of the imperial slaughterhouse (see opposite) and the director's residence were located in the imposing Palacete do Matadouro, now known as Palacete Princesa Isabel. Also dating from 1881, the neoclassical building's gardens were designed by French urban planner François Marie Glaziou, who was responsible for renovating the Passeio Público (see p. 120). The enormous fig trees surrounding the palace are from this period,

as are the imperious palm trees at the entrance. Shortly after its inauguration, it was converted into a school. Over the years, the building fell into disrepair and even caught fire. Since its restoration in the 1980s, it has housed a cultural centre and NOPH, a community initiative initially conceived to conserve historic buildings in Santa Cruz.

For the benefit of slaughterhouse employees and their families, a workers' village was built next to the palace. Today the houses, although still occupied, are not what they once were.

The Santa Cruz Ecomuseum, originally known as the Ecomuseu do Quarteirão Cultural do Matadouro, is the city's first ecomuseum, a concept that originated in France in the 1970s. In these new "contemporary museums", the idea of "heritage" has replaced that of the "collection of objects" of traditional museums. Similarly, the notions of "participating community" and "terrain/sense of place" have taken over from "public/ visitor" and "building/headquarters", respectively. The Santa Cruz museum was recognised in 1992 for NOPH's work, on the occasion of the first International Meeting of Ecomuseums held in Rio de Janeiro.

MARKER NUMBER 7 OF THE ESTRADA REAL ❽ (ROYAL ROAD)

Opposite Paço Imperial de Santa Cruz
Praça Ruão
Santa Cruz

> *Route linking the imperial palaces of São Cristóvão and Santa Cruz*

I n the middle of the lawn at Praça Ruão, facing what was the Imperial Palace of Santa Cruz (now Battalion Villagran Cabrita, see p. 246), stands a modest stone marker. It is not far from a copy of the large wooden cross erected by the Jesuits in the 16th century. This is one of the twelve route markers of the Royal Road of Santa Cruz, which indicated the distance between the palaces of Santa Cruz and São Cristóvão.

According to researchers from the Núcleo de Orientação e Pesquisa Histórica (NOPH – Centre for Historical Orientation and Research) of Santa Cruz, the marker of Praça Ruão, which was not originally located here, is one of three still in existence. It also has something rather unique: you can read the symbols of the Empire and the Republic, respectively PI (Pedro I) and FN (Fazenda Nacional) and its number (7) and a reference to the year 1826.

The other two known markers are number 11, also in Santa Cruz, in the square that bears its name; and number 10 at Paciência, near the BRT bus terminal.

The route has existed since the time of the Jesuits – it was also known as the Jesuit Route. It connected Fazenda Santa Cruz to Morro do Castelo (see p. 61), site of the Jesuit College. Over time, the route changed its name: first, Caminho de Minas (as it went as far as Minas Gerais, where the gold sent to Portugal came from), and then Estrada Real, before becoming Estrada Imperial de Santa Cruz. Sections of the route are now main city thoroughfares.

DOM PEDRO I, HIS MISTRESS AND THE ORIGIN OF THE NAME "PACIÊNCIA"

History and legend meet in the name of the railway station, opened in 1887, and the surrounding district – Paciência (Patience). This was the site of Fazenda do Mato da Paciência, probably the country's oldest sugar plantation. There is also evidence that when Dom Pedro I and his court were on their way to Santa Cruz palace (see p. 246), they stopped there to rest their horses. The story goes that on reaching their resting place, the emperor mounted a waiting horse to join the Marquise de Santos (Domitila de Castro Canto e Melo, 1797–1867) from the nearby estate. His courtiers grew tired of waiting and kept asking the coachmen when they could resume their journey. Knowing the habits of Dom Pedro and the time he spent in the arms of his famous mistress, the coachmen invariably replied: "Patience, patience, we must have patience ..."

CAPELA MAGDALENA

9

6024 Estrada do Mato Alto, Guaratiba
• R$120 per person, including lunch or dinner, concert and entry to the museum
• Visits on reservation only – avoid Friday evenings (massive traffic jams guaranteed, coming from Rio)
• Tel: (21) 2410-7183
• E-mail: contato_capelamagdalena@yahoo.com.br

A unique moment in a unique place

The Magdalena Chapel, an hour's drive from Rio city centre, towards the end of Barra de Tijuca, is unique.

The chapel, designed by Roberto de Regina, is also a concert venue, a restaurant and a small private museum of miniature reproductions of trains, planes, boats, castles, churches and famous buildings around the world.

Roberto, a former anaesthetist, is an amazing character. As he says himself, he's spent much of his life putting people to sleep. Now he wakes them up with his sensitivity, generosity and creativity. Indeed, he's done almost everything himself: painting frescoes on the chapel walls, building the harpsichord on which he gives concerts of Baroque music and designing most of the museum's 500 objects.

Although you can join an existing group (always call to book), we recommend getting together ten to twelve people (or more) to have the place

to yourselves. In the words of "maestro" Roberto, who also prefers small groups, the conversation flows much better in an intimate setting.

Finally, for those for whom Renaissance music isn't an overwhelming passion, be assured that Roberto's spirit and the quality of the music will mean that you have a great time.

We strongly advise spending the whole day at the site: lunch at the Capela, then beach (Grumari or Guaratiba's secret beaches, see p. 254) and dinner nearby (such as the excellent Bira) or vice versa: beach for lunch, then dinner at the Capela.
The renowned Burle Marx garden is another good and relatively nearby choice.

TRANSCARIOCA TRAIL TO THE WILD BEACHES ❿ OF GRUMARI

Trail starts at Barra de Guaratiba, Rua Siqueira Parlon
• Tel: (21) 2410-1382 (Parque Natural Municipal do Grumari)
• Distance: 8 km (one way, Guaratiba-Grumari round trip)
• Duration: 4 hours (one way, Guaratiba-Grumari round trip)
• Free

Deserted urban beaches

When dreaming of deserted beaches, the Caribbean or the South Pacific immediately springs to mind. But you don't need to go that far. Rio de Janeiro has five deserted beaches that are all accessible from the Transcarioca trail – its starting point coincides with the entrance to these beaches.

The path to the beaches of Búzios (not to be confused with the small seaside town east of Rio), Perigoso, Meio, Funda and Inferno is easy and well-marked by wooden arrows interspersed with the yellow Transcarioca markers painted on trees and rocks. This signage, and the cleanliness of the beaches, are thanks to the efforts of the Grumari Municipal Natural Park managers and the NGO Amigos do Perigoso (Friends of Perigoso). They have adopted this stretch of the Transcarioca trail and regularly organise volunteer clean-up operations to get rid of any rubbish.

During an expedition to Rio in 1833, the English botanist Sir Charles James Fox Bunbury wrote: "The beaches near Rio are usually lined with rows of evergreen shrubs, mostly Cayenne cherry (Pitanga) …". Some two centuries later, the wild beaches of Guaratiba haven't changed.

The walk alternates between closed forest sections (replanted in the 1990s), rocky headlands and many white sand beaches. Don't forget to take a hat, sunscreen and plenty of water.

Before reaching the first stretch of sand, a worthwhile detour (by a well-marked trail) to the Telegraph Mirador offers a spectacular view of Rio de Janeiro. After Praia do Perigoso, you can climb up to the path again and resume your walk. The path, which goes round the headland, then takes you to the beaches of Meio, Funda and Inferno. In fifteen minutes you'll reach Praia do Meio, which has a freshwater spring. From there, carry on to the top of the hill at the far end of the beach. Another fifteen minutes and you'll emerge at Praia do Funda, which is usually deserted. From there to Praia do Inferno, it's just a five-minute climb from the headland.

After Inferno, follow the yellow markers to join the Transcarioca Grumari trail.

A STRETCH THAT ENDS AT GRUMARI

After about 8 km, a stretch of the Transcarioca trail ends at Grumari.

To get back to the starting point, you'll have to retrace your steps or travel by road between Grumari and Barra de Guaratiba.

If you prefer the second option, it's best to take two cars: leave one at the end of the trail and the other at the start, so that you can easily get back to the first.

It's said that when he needed to make difficult decisions, former Governor Leonel Brizola took a helicopter to Praia do Inferno to reflect in peace.

STATUE OF A FOOTBALL PLAYER　⓫

240 Rua Fonseca
• Train: SuperVia at Central do Brasil; Bangu station

> **Brazil's first football match**

To the left of the main entrance of Bangu Shopping, near the mall car park, is a bronze statue of a man holding a football, arm raised in celebration. The inscription on the little fountain below claims this as the site of Brazil's first football match.

This statue is a tribute to the Scot, Thomas Donohoe, who organised a six-a-side match on 9 September 1894. The improvised pitch was on a vacant lot in front of the Fábrica de Tecidos Bangu (Bangu textile factory), with four stakes for goalposts. The reduced number of players was no problem for Donohoe and his teammates, nor was the absence of team jerseys or stopwatch. The point was to have a good time.

Donohoe, a dyer in a textile factory near Glasgow, Scotland, went to Rio de Janeiro in May 1894 to work in the new textile factory that had opened a year earlier. Arriving at Bangu, after an hour and a half's train ride from the centre of Rio, he found a town with only one street and less than a thousand residents. He also discovered that there were no football teams in the neighbourhood and that Brazilians knew nothing about the game – a disappointment for this 31-year-old athlete who'd been a keen player back home.

His family (wife and two young children) arrived at the port of Rio on 5 September 1894, with a special package for Donohoe in their luggage: a football. While still on the train to Bangu, Donohoe took something out of his suitcase that the other passengers thought was just a few strips of leather sewn together. To everyone's surprise, Donohoe pumped up the piece of leather into a ball and began to play with it right inside the carriage!

"Seu Danau", as he was called by the factory workers, defended the colours of Bangu Atlético Clube, which he'd helped to found in 1904. He died in October 1925.

The Bangu factory closed in February 2004, after decades spent playing a prominent role in the economic, social and cultural life of the region and of the city. Three years later, a commercial centre named Bangu Shopping restored the building's listed façade and opened for business.

As a result of Donohoe's improvisations and the lack of official rules (jerseys, stopwatch, goal markers, number of players, pitch dimensions) during the September 1894 match at Bangu, some consider that the country's first authentic football match was held in April 1895, seven months after Donohoe's, as it followed the Association Football rules set by Charles Miller from São Paulo.

BUMBA-MEU-BOI HOUSE/MUSEUM ⓬

Associação Raízes de Gericinó
80 Estrada do Gericinó, casa 3-A, Bangu
• Open daily, for reservations call (21) 3465-3959
• Bus: 398, 366, 364, 2336 (Avenida Brasil stop – after the Coca-Cola plant – take first street on right and walk about 150 m)
• Admission: R$5

Souvenir of Maranhão Bumba-meu-boi performances

This small building with ornamental railings on its veranda, just at the entrance to an apartment block for around 300 residents, stands on a square of bare lawn. It's home to the small Bumba-meu-boi museum (see box) and the headquarters of the non-profit association Raízes de Gericinó (Roots of Gericinó, a working-class district of Rio), born of the collective struggle for the right to home ownership in the Brazilian state of Maranhão.

The whole place is a living museum: apart from displaying the symbols and costumes used annually during local performances of Bumba-meu-boi, Raízes de Gericinó defends the cultural roots of the Maranhão region that persist in the neighbourhood. It offers clothing and accessories workshops, crafts, dance and reading for the children of the community, to preserve the Bumba-meu-boi tradition.

Everything is informal but structured. The virtually family-run project goes back to the arrival in Rio of the Merces family from Maranhão: Seu José, Dona Rosa and six of their children. Despite the hard life endured by the poor migrants, the Merces liked to party and soon organised large gatherings with music from the Northeast and typical dishes. These events gradually won new followers in the neighbourhood, families like themselves fighting for the ownership of their lodgings and to earn a living with dignity.

In 2011, homesick for Maranhão Bumba-meu-boi, the Merces held their first performance, which they called "Bumba-meu-boi, Star of Gericinó". Gradually the group expanded beyond simple family ties. The costumes and accessories, which had been brought from Maranhão, were now made by the community through the work of the Raízes association. Every year in July, the Star of Gericinó festival takes place in the little square by the museum, amid music, dancing and many local dishes.

WHAT IS BUMBA-MEU-BOI?

Bumba-meu-boi, one of the richest representations of Brazilian folklore, is widespread in the North and Northeast regions. Originating in the 18th century, this performance – known by different names in different states – is a kind of popular opera, fusing dance, music, theatre and circus. The story is built around a rich farmer who owns a splendid ox that is impounded and dies, but is resurrected. It all ends in a huge party.

MUSEU BISPO DE ROSÁRIO ⑬

3400 Estrada Rodrigues Caldas
Jacarepaguá
• Open Tuesday to Saturday 10am–5pm
• Tel: (21) 3432-2402 • http://museubispodorosario.com

A genial "paranoid schizophrenic" artist

Arthur Bispo de Rosário (1909–1989), a major figure of *art brut* ("raw" or "outsider" art), is certainly the artist whose work best reflects the approach of the great Brazilian psychiatrist Nise da Silveira (see Museu de Imagens do Inconsciente, p. 295). His creations are regularly shown in major exhibitions of international contemporary art.

In 1938, Bispo suffered a psychotic breakdown during which he became aware of his mission on Earth: recreating the universe in a form presentable to God to obtain redemption at the Last Judgment. He was arrested, hospitalised and diagnosed as a paranoid schizophrenic. He was finally admitted to Colônia Juliano Moreira, a psychiatric facility in Rio de Janeiro, where he remained until his death (see opposite). This artist, who never attended art school or even underwent occupational therapy (see opposite), has left behind a considerable body of 800 catalogued works in the museum that bears his name, opened in 2000.

He spent most of his life unwittingly exchanging ideas from his cell with the major currents of 20th-century art, from Marcel Duchamp's work on *arte povera* ("poor" art) through to conceptual art, at a time when Brazilian neo-concretism was breaking with all traditional media.

Bispo himself used mixed media. His works were created from found objects of everyday life, such as buttons, bottles, paper, cardboard, hospital sheets, various utensils, rubber boots or simple pieces of wood … His sculptures and other objects are sometimes covered with richly textured embroidered fabrics. He also made clothes such as his "Annunciation outfit" (the best known), which he intended to wear on Judgment Day, but also banners, boats, cars, a boxing ring and so on.

The museum has a policy of inviting contemporary artists to enter a dialogue with the work of Bispo de Rosário. This has resulted in a series of high-quality temporary exhibitions, justifying the addition of "Arte Contemporânea" to the museum's name.

COLÔNIA JULIANO MOREIRA: SCIENCE, HISTORY AND NATURE

Less than five minutes' drive from the museum, Colônia Juliano Moreira (Taquara district, 3400 Estrada Rodrigues Caldas, Jacarepaguá) is a psychiatric institution set up in the first half of the 20th century by Juliano Moreira (1873–1932), a pioneer of Brazilian psychiatry. He was known for his work on humanising treatment and rehabilitation through work, particularly on agricultural estates.

With nearly 80 km² of protected grounds, the site still houses psychiatric units and a scientific campus inspired by the Institut Pasteur. You can discover many historical links as well as some exceptional natural surroundings. The premises are on the site of the former sugar plantation of Nossa Senhora dos Remédios (Our Lady of the Remedies), a Christian martyr who was dismembered in 1664. There's still a church of the same name (19th century), an 18th-century former aqueduct and many buildings that are unfortunately in poor condition. An enjoyable walk through the Parque Estadual da Pedra Branca (White Stone State Park) leads to Colônia's magnificent *cachoeira* (waterfall).

"AÇUDE" TRAIL

Trail starts at junction of Estrada da Princesa Imperial and Estrada do Visconde do Bom Retiro (in Tijuca forest)
- Duration: two hours
- Museu do Açude: 764 Estrada do Açude, Alto da Boa Vista
- Admission free (museum closed Tuesdays)
- Tel: (21) 3433-499 (museum) / 2491-1700

> **Cascatinha waterfall as you've never seen it before**

All Cariocas know Tijuca forest and have already heard of the Açude museum. What few know is that the two are connected by one of the most beautiful stretches of the Transcarioca trail. The path, which is maintained by the group of volunteers, is fully signposted with yellow markers that are the hallmarks of Transcarioca. The hike takes about two hours (starting near Os Esquilos restaurant and ending near Cascatinha) and is full of history, beautiful scenery and local wildlife.

The trail was used by Raymundo Ottoni de Castro Maya, former owner of the residence that is now the Açude museum, to reach Tijuca forest, which he managed from 1943 to 1947. Perhaps that's why it's so wide and well defined.

Between the forest and the museum, you'll pass through Alto do Cruzeiro, a place with a large wooden cross where Mass was held for the slaves in the days when the region was covered with coffee plantations. You can then climb up an observation tower and onto a bridge where, with luck, you'll spot toucans and hawks.

At Açude museum, you'll come across Castro Maya's former riding stables, nowadays home to a fantastic installation of artworks by Hélio Oiticica.

Continuing the walk for another hour or so is well worth the effort as you can visit Castro Maya's former residence – it's decorated with Portuguese *azulejos* that belonged to the Marquis of Marialva and has a Dutch fireplace carved at Pernambuco by Maurício de Nassau, among other fine works of art collected by Castro Maya. Even without going into the museum you can enjoy his garden, which is full of artworks and antique pots, along with modern installations acquired by the present management.

After rounding the main house and going through the stables, the Transcarioca climbs up again into Tijuca forest along a path that corresponds to the former boundaries of the property – you can still see markers with the initials CM (Castro Maya) stamped on them. Before heading down towards Praça Afonso Vizeu, there's one last gem to be discovered: a wooden deck with the Cascatinha viewpoint. From there magnificent views of the forest open out – no traces of civilisation, just the green of the Atlantic forest surrounding the 30 m waterfall of Cascatinha de Taunay.

TRANSCARIOCA TRAIL, FROM ALTO DA BOA VISTA TO MESA DO IMPERADOR ⓯

Trailhead: Praça Afonso Viseu (Alto da Boa Vista)
- Distance: 8.2 km (one way)
- Duration: 3¹/₂ hours (one way)
- Admission free
- Tel: (21) 2491-1700 (Floresta da Tijuca, Parque Nacional da Tijuca)

360-degree views of Rio

This little-known trail connects the mountains of Tijuca and Carioca by the Morro do Queimado ridge. The lengthy, steep and tiring hike is still worth every drop of sweat but be sure to take plenty of water with you. On the way, you'll pass a dozen watchtowers from where you can gaze down successively on Barra da Tijuca, Pedra da Gávea, the Zona Norte with Sierra dos Órgãos in the distance, Corcovado, Sugarloaf Mountain and Rodrigo de Freitas lagoon, from various angles that only this trail can offer.

The route is fully signposted with yellow Transcarioca markers. The hike begins at the gate of Tijuca Forest National Park, Praça Afonso Viseu, in Alto da Boa Vista. Follow the yellow markers painted on poles, cross Rua Boa Vista and ascend Rua Amado Nervo. Arriving at the national park gates, go into the forest by the wooden steps to the right. Be warned that it's a long climb through the Atlantic rainforest.

After about forty minutes, you'll reach a fork in the track. To the right, about ten minutes away, lies the viewpoint of Freira with its unrivalled panorama of Pedra da Gávea. The detour is well worth it.

Back on the main section of the Transcarioca trail, the climb continues and gradually offers the best views of the city.

After three hours' walk you'll reach the heights of Morro do Queimado, where the panorama is truly sublime. From this point, the trail is almost all downhill. It then continues through the forest and over a small hill before descending to a flat trail where you turn right.

You'll now find yourself following a former tram route opened in 1857 to link the botanical gardens and the city centre. The construction company dynamited half the route to widen it sufficiently for carriages to pass between the rocks, but work was never completed as the company went bankrupt.

Following the tram route, you'll reach the top of the steps leading to the Mesa do Imperador (Emperor's Table), where Dom Pedro II organised picnics with the royal family. From there, hardier souls can carry on as far as the Vista Chinesa (Chinese View) or the Solar da Imperatriz (Empress's Manor). Otherwise we suggest taking two cars, leaving one at the Mesa do Imperador and the other in Praça Afonso Viseu, so you can easily get back to the first.

THE MYSTERIOUS INSCRIPTION ON PEDRA DA GÁVEA

At 842 m above sea level, Pedra da Gávea was the first Carioca mountain spotted by the sailors of the Portuguese expedition under Captain Gaspar de Lemos: on 1 January 1502 they saw the form of a topsail (*gávea*) and named the rock after it. For some, the theory (disputed) of the presence of Phoenicians in Brazil, is that Pedra da Gávea was shaped by Phoenician navigators who reached these shores around 1000 BC. According to a theory advanced by Robertus Comtaeus Nortmannus (1644) and George Horn (1652), the Phoenicians saw the outline of a sphinx in the rock.

This theme was taken up in 1928 by the Austrian Ludwig Schwennhagen, who taught history and philosophy in Northeast Brazil, and especially by Bernardo da Silva Ramos, the "Brazilian Champollion", in 1930. This writer discovered inscriptions on the face of Pedra da Gávea in which he identified (and rendered in Portuguese) the Phoenician letters that compose, from right to left: TYRO PHENICIA, BADEZIR, PRIMOGÊNITO DE JETHBAAL (Phoenician of Tyre, Badezir, first son of Jethbaal). In 1954, Professor Henrique José de Souza, founder of the Sociedade Teosófica no Brasil (Theosophical Society of Brazil) came up with a revised version: "TYRO PHENICIA, JETHBAAL, PRIMOGÊNITO DE BADEZIR (Phoenician of Tyre, Jethbaal, first son of Badezir). Other people maintain that these letters are simply natural manifestations of weathered stone.

Professor de Souza delved deep into the mystery of Pedra da Gávea and its relation to the Phoenician history of Brazil. According to him, the exiled king of Tyre (capital of Phoenicia), *Baal-Zir* or *Badezir* came here with his twin children *Yet-Baal-Bey* and *Yet-Baal-Bel*. (Some think the name Brazil is derived from Badezir, rather than from the national tree *pau-brasil* – *pau* meaning wood, and *brasil* meaning red/ember-like in Portuguese).

One day, on the way across Guanabara bay from Niteroi, their boat went straight to the bottom in a storm and they were all drowned. The bodies were recovered and placed at the heart of Pedra da Gávea (*Metaracanga* in the Tupi language), which in a way became their tomb. For millennia, the funerary remains rested inside the monolith in a cavity dug by human hands, and then mysteriously disappeared. The phrase "Phoenician of Tyre, Jethbaal, first son of Badezir" would then have been a posthumous tribute from the king Badezir to his elder son. It would have been the monarch's effigy carved on the face of Pedra da Gávea, in the guise of a bearded and helmeted old man. A huge white slab, rising up behind the Pedra on the São Conrado side, marks the supposed entrance to the interior of the monolith. Emperor Dom Pedro II of Brazil had himself depicted as a sphinx in a 19th-century engraving.

TIJUCA
SÃO CRISTÓVÃO
ZONA NORTE

CENTRO MUNICIPAL DE REFERÊNCIA DA MÚSICA CARIOCA ARTUR DA TÁVOLA ❶

824 Rua Conde de Bonfim
Tijuca
• R$20 (full price) or R$10 (half price) (for concerts – exhibitions are usually free)
• Metro: Uruguai
• Open Tuesday, Wednesday and Sunday 10am–6pm, Thursday and Saturday 10am–8pm
• Ongoing programmes for children at weekends
• Tel: (21) 3238-3831 / 3238-3880
• creferenciadamusicacarioca.blogspot.com

Rio's home of music

From Tijuca's Praça Saens Peña, heading up Rua Conde de Bonfim towards the Usina or Alto da Boavista neighbourhoods, there's a surprise in store at the corner of Rua Garibaldi. Here, in contrast to the monotonous succession of buildings and commercial establishments bordering most of the route, an ancient and imposing French-style medieval mansion stands out.

This small palace, built in 1921, is one of the few examples of its kind left in the neighbourhood. It was designed by the architect Gaspar José de Souza Reis as the home of Portuguese merchant Manoel Vieira Júnior. It was subsequently owned by an Italian called Mário Bianchi, a successful businessman in the transport sector.

Although the building's architectural beauty leaves no one indifferent, it has not always been so. Neglected for over twenty years, the fabric of the building began to deteriorate. Its prospects started to improve in the late 1980s, when a group of residents and regulars of the Bar da Dona Maria (traditional samba venue, opposite the mansion) launched a campaign to have the building listed before converting it into a cultural centre devoted to music. The initiative was successful and in 1995, Palacete Garibaldi was listed as local heritage. After long and extensive renovations, the Artur da Távola Municipal Centre for Carioca Music moved there in June 2007. This space is intended to preserve the city's rich musical heritage.

The ground-floor rooms are reserved for exhibitions, workshops and concerts of classical music. The floor above is reserved for the administration. Besides its verandas and balconies, the place also has a welcoming winter garden and beautiful stained-glass doors and windows.

In addition to the original mansion, the centre has the use of two annexes
built during the renovations: a concert hall with a capacity of 161, a small
administration building and three rooms for workshops and music lessons.
A former garage houses a recording studio and three additional workshops.

Finally, there's a pretty garden with a little jetty at the far end: a reminder of
the time when the Maracanã river was clean and navigable.

OMBRELLINO OF SÃO SEBASTIÃO DOS CAPUCHINHOS

❷

266 Rua Haddock Lobo
Tijuca
• Open daily until 7pm
• Metro: Afonso Pena
• Tel: (21) 2204-7900 / 2204-7904 / 2204-7905

The forgotten symbol of basilicas

To the right of the altar of the basilica church of St Sebastian of the Capuchins, the discreet canopy resembling an umbrella, whose wooden frame is covered with striped red and yellow silk in the colours of the Vatican Pontifical government, is known as an *umbraculum* or *ombrellino*. These colours have themselves been inherited from ancient Rome, where they were those of the Roman Senate.

Historically, the canopy was a tent that sheltered the patriarch and royalty in the Old Testament. The symbols of canopy and bell (tintinnabulum) are reserved for basilicas and signify their link with the pope. The canopy is half open when in a minor basilica (as here) and fully open in major basilicas (see below and *Secret Rome* in this series of guides). During papal visits, however, it is also fully open in minor basilicas.

WHAT IS A BASILICA?

In the Roman Empire, the basilica was the palace where the king (*basileus*) dispensed justice. After the Edict of Milan (313) that brought Christians out of hiding and put an end to persecution, Emperor Constantine had four churches built in Rome, known as "major" basilicas, which he donated to the pope. These are St Peter's in Vatican City, on the supposed site of the martyrdom of St Peter; St Paul Outside the Walls, on the scene of the martyrdom of St Paul; St Maria Maggiore, the first church in Christendom dedicated to Mary; and St John Lateran, in honour of the apostle "whom Jesus loved". The Archbasilica of St John in the Lateran is the seat of the pope and the Cathedral of Rome, "mother and head of all the churches of the city and the world". All other basilicas in Rome or elsewhere are classified as "minor": they have privileges such as the protection of the Holy See linked with one of the four major basilicas. Nowadays a church can be honoured with the title of basilica by papal decree, according to its spiritual influence and exemplary daily practices.

THREE MAJOR RELICS OF RIO DE JANEIRO AT ST SEBASTIAN'S

By a decision of Pope Francis on 1 November 2015 (commemorating the date of the last Mass in São Sebastião do Castelo church, demolished in 1922 along with the *morro* of the same name – see p. 61), São Sebastião dos Capuchinhos became a minor basilica, to highlight its important role. It houses three of the city's major relics previously kept in São Sebastião do Castelo church – the city's foundation stone from 1565 (left of the nave); the remains of the city founder, Estácio de Sá, who died in 1567 (in front of the altar); and the historical image (1563) of St Sebastian, patron saint of the city (see p. 127).

Every year on 20 January (St Sebastian's feast day), this image joins the procession to the Catedral Metropolitana in the city centre. The rest of the year, the image is not on public view.

MUSICAL SIDEWALKS OF VILA ISABEL ③

Boulevard 28 de Setembro (from Praça Maracanã to Praça Barão de Drumond)
Vila Isabel
• Bus: from Zona Sul (432, 433, 438, 439); Centro (222, etc.)

A musical neighbourhood

The musical sidewalks of Vila Isabel – inaugurated in 1964 by Governor Carlos Lacerda as part of preparations for the commemoration of the city's fourth centenary the following year – are found on both sides of the main thoroughfare, Avenida / Boulevard 28 de Setembro. They are an ode to Brazilian popular music: engraved on the black and white Portuguese paving are the scores of various popular songs plus images of instruments.

The project was the brainchild of architect Orlando Magdalena, a local resident, and met with the enthusiastic approval of the authorities. The musical scores were divided into pages to match the width of the sidewalks, and drawings of instruments such as the guitar, *cavaquinho* (small Portuguese guitar), piano and *pandeiro* (percussion) were dotted among them. Another architect, Hugo Ribeiro, helped to design these instruments and paid tribute to Noel Rosa, songwriter, singer and guitar or mandolin player, by affixing his initials to a guitar. The choice of songs was made by the creator of the project and Almirante, a renowned expert in Brazilian popular music.

The series of songs, twenty in all, starts with the city's anthem, *Cidade maravilhosa* (Marvellous City) by André Filho, in Praça Maracanã. Among the others are *Ó abre alas* (the "abre alas" is the lorry opening the Carnaval parade) by Chiquinha Gonzaga, the first song composed for the carnival; *Pelo telefone* (By Telephone) by Donga and Mauro de Almeida, the first recorded samba (1918); *Feitiço da Vila* (The Charm of Vila) by Noel Rosa, composer par excellence of Vila Isabel and leading light of 1930s Brazilian popular music; *Ave Maria* by Erotildes Campos and Jonas Neves, in front of Nossa Senhora de Lourdes basilica; *Jura* (Oath) by Sinhô and J. B. Silva; and *Carinhoso* (Affectionate) by Pixinguinha and Antônio da Rocha Viana. The last song is *Renascer das cinzas* (Reborn from the Ashes) by Martinho da Vila, in Praça Barão de Drumond. The musical sidewalks were listed by Rio City Hall in April 1999.

There is another tribute to Brazilian music at Vila Isabel: a statue of Noel Rosa in Praça Maracanã, at the entrance to the neighbourhood. Noel Rosa is shown sitting on a bar stool with a cigarette between his fingers, a waiter in attendance. On the table beside him stand a bottle of beer, a glass and a sheet, also in bronze, bearing the words of the samba *Conversa de botequim* (Bistro Conversation). Beside him, an empty chair invites visitors to sit down for a selfie. A curious feature of the statue is that the young man's features are based on those of Rosa's father. Unveiled on 22 March 1996, it was designed by Joás Pereira Passos from Paraíba state.

STATUE OF BELLINI   ④

Gate D of Mário Filho stadium (Maracanã)
Rua Professor Eurico Rabelo
• Metro: Maracanã

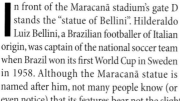

Statue with different features to its namesake

In front of the Maracanã stadium's gate D stands the "statue of Bellini". Hilderaldo Luiz Bellini, a Brazilian footballer of Italian origin, was captain of the national soccer team when Brazil won its first World Cup in Sweden in 1958. Although the Maracanã statue is named after him, not many people know (or even notice) that its features bear not the slightest resemblance to Bellini.

Most of those involved in this episode are now dead, so it's difficult to explain what happened. In a 2010 interview, the player's widow recalled that her husband had twice asked for the sculptor Matheus Fernandes "because of his athletic stature and the position of his hand".

Some people argue that the statue's face is that of singer Francisco Alves, aka "King of the Voice", who was very popular in the 1950s. But it also bears a strong resemblance to journalist Hamilton Sbarra, who in an interview with a newspaper at the time revealed that the sculptor had asked him for a photo, saying he needed "a face with a Graeco-Roman profile, like mine". Although suspicious, Sbarra complied.

The inscription on the base of the statue (9 m tall and weighing 3 tonnes), which was unveiled on 13 November 1960, makes no reference to Bellini but is simply dedicated "To the World Champions". But over time, people started to refer to it as the "statue of Bellini" and that's what everybody calls it now.

The difference between the official and popular versions of events seems typical of this stadium, named after journalist Mário Filho but known worldwide as the Maracanã, or "Maraca" to keen Carioca fans. It was built for the 1950 World Cup and opened on 16 June of that year, with a friendly match between the Rio de Janeiro and São Paulo teams in which the first goal was scored by the Carioca player Didi. Top scorer at the Maracanã is Zico, idol of the Flamengo club: 333 goals in 435 games. Pelé scored his thousandth goal there too, in 1969.

Macaranã is a word of Tupí origin, meaning "like a *chocalho*" (the sound of birds of the Psittacidae subfamily *maracana*, which includes species such as parrot, macaw and parakeet). Before the stadium was built, the site was home to numerous bird species.

The stadium was once the largest in the world (for the final of the 1950 World Cup, it hosted over 199,000 spectators, many standing). It is still the largest in Brazil, with a capacity of 78,800 (all seated).

ASSOCIAÇÃO DE FERROMODELISMO DO RIO DE JANEIRO (AFERJ)

⑤

Former Leopoldina train station
Rua Francisco Eugênio – Praça da Bandeira
• Room 106, ground floor
• Saturdays approx. 9am–5pm
• Metro: São Cristóvão
• Admission free

"

> *Model railway in an abandoned station*

The model railway track of the former Leopoldina train station, closed to passenger traffic since 2001, is one of Rio's great secrets.

Every Saturday, from about 9am to 5pm, the heavy metal gates at the entrance to the abandoned station are opened so that the thirty members of the Model Railway Association of Rio de Janeiro can indulge their passion. They run their miniature locomotives and wagons around a network that has about 300 m of track over a 55 m² surface. The association, which was set up in 1986, also has a small repair workshop for members. They pay R$150 each to register and R$30 per month for the right to operate their little trains.

The venue is open to the public and members are usually delighted to share their enthusiasm with visitors who drop in.

You'll learn that the circuit has five different tracks, each independent from the other: once the train is on the network, the only thing the operator can change is its speed. And, as in real life, they'll run a high-speed train faster than a freight train.

The AFERJ also offers the exciting possibility of visiting the remains of the former Barão de Mauá station, with its rusted carriages still on the tracks, the old ticket booths and original waiting rooms … Opened in 1926, the station was designed by Scottish architect Robert Prentice.

WHEN WILL BRAZIL HAVE A PROPER RAILWAY NETWORK?

Having developed mainly to serve a coffee-based economy, the Brazilian rail passenger network is now almost non-existent: the only viable stretch is between Belo Horizonte and Vitoria, far from being the country's most essential route. In a country that frequently suffers from apocalyptic traffic jams on the way out of the major cities, this lack of trains (even to connect the main cities) is a scandal. The quality of life is at stake. And it's an urgent question for the country.

BAIRRO SANTA GENOVEVA

446 Rua São Cristóvão
• Metro: São Cristóvão
• Visits only on invitation from a local resident (ask at the entrance) or
during Mass (very irregular)

**A
mini-Montmartre
in Rio**

An attractive gate alongside number 446 Rua São Cristóvão bears the inscription "Bairro Santa Genoveva". If you're lucky enough to meet a resident at the gate, and they agree to "invite" you to visit this private neighbourhood, you'll have the privilege of strolling around a group of a hundred little houses built by the Viscount of Moraes. Leader of the Portuguese colony in Brazil, Eurico José Pereira de Moraes established this workers' village on a small *morro* in 1917 close to the Persian column in front of the Conde de Linhares Military Museum (see p. 283).

Although the area has the reputation of being a small Montmartre, it is rather a small St Geneviève (Santa Genoveva). The Montagne Sainte-Geneviève in Paris, a hill on the Left Bank, is, as here, much smaller than Montmartre.

The most charming spot is right at the top of the *morro*, where a

small square and an attractive tree overlook a church that is only open on the last Saturday of the month. The church, a scaled-down copy of Sacré-Coeur (Basilica of the Sacred Heart in Montmartre, Paris), was built to fulfil a promise made by the viscount to the patron saint of Paris (St Geneviève) concerning his wife's health.

All the streets in the neighbourhood (Rua Savero, Rua Geronia, Praça Nanterre, Rua Lutécia, etc.) refer to St Geneviève: born in Nanterre near Paris in 423, she was the only daughter of Severus (Savero), a probably Romanised Frank, and Géroncia (Geronia), a woman of Greek origin. Paris was known as Lutèce in St Geneviève's time.

COLUNA DE PERSEPOLIS ❼

Praça Pedro II
São Cristóvão
• Metro: São Cristóvão

Forgotten column of Persepolis

The column in Praça Pedro II, at the end of Rua São Cristóvão, opposite the entrance to Conde de Linhares military museum, often goes unnoticed.

The 9-metre-high column was a gift from Iranian President Mahmoud Ahmadinejad on the occasion of the 2012 Rio climate change conference. It is a replica of a column that still stands in one of the throne rooms (*apadana*) at Persepolis – once a capital city of the Achaemenid Persian empire and now a UNESCO World Heritage site. The city was founded in 521 BC by the Persian King Darius the Great, long before the Muslim era.

The column is surmounted by two opposing bull's heads. In the Persian tradition, this animal is an image of strength and power, protection and defence, and a personification of royal authority.

At the foot of the column, two bas-reliefs show a lion devouring a bull. In Persian tradition, this scene symbolises the New Year (Nowruz, between 20 and 22 March, the spring equinox), when the constellation Leo is in the zenith, while that of Taurus heads south. Nowruz marks the beginning of agricultural activity after the winter period.

Finally, an inscription in English and Portuguese recalls a dialogue between King Darius and Ahura Mazda, the Zoroastrian god worshipped in Persia before the introduction of Islam. Zoroastrianism is still practised in Iran and parts of India. Note the translation error in the Portuguese version of this dialogue, which recalls the benefits of virtuous conduct: *desejo que, se ele fizer o mal, que ele não seja punido* ("I wish that he who does evil should not be punished"). The phrase should be the other way round (English version is correct).

ENTRANCE TO RIO ZOO ⑧

Parque Quinta da Boa Vista
São Cristóvão
• Metro: São Cristóvão

**The gift of
an English duke
in artificial stone**

Not much attention is paid to the entrance to Rio Zoo (Jardim Zoólogico). Yet it's the only South American example of Coade stone, an artificial construction material of English origin (see opposite). This gateway was the gift of General Hugh Percy, 2nd Duke of Northumberland, for the marriage of Dom Pedro I and the future empress, Maria Leopoldina of Austria (1817).

John Johnston, the English architect responsible for the renovation of São Cristóvão palace at the time, set the gateway at the entrance of what became the Imperial Palace, as seen in the engraving below. It remained there until at least the 1860s before being moved to the zoo.

The gateway is a copy of a Robert Adam design that graces Syon House, the Duke of Northumberland's former residence on the outskirts of London.

> See overleaf for more illustrations of the former site of the São Cristóvão gateway and of Syon House.

THE MYSTERY OF COADE STONE

Coade stone (*Lithodipyra* or "twice-fired stone"], little known outside the UK, is a ceramic "artificial stone" named after Eleanor Coade junior (1733–1821).

The material owes its success to the property boom that London was experiencing at that time. As most buildings were of brick, the architects made wide use of Coade stone to embellish their façades.

The mix contains finely ground, fired potters' clay that can be cast very easily to produce statues, architectural decorations and garden ornaments, allowing very fine detail and exact copies. The moulds can be used over and over again, greatly reducing manufacturing costs.

Another important advantage of Coade stone is its extreme durability. It is resistant to the elements and the corrosive urban air – examples over 200 years old still show no obvious signs of wear or deterioration.

Eleanor was both a brilliant businesswoman and a very fine sculptor, so she not only ran one of the most successful 18th-century companies but she also created many of the original sculptures from which the moulds were taken. She bought a pottery in Lambeth, on the site where the Royal Festival Hall now stands, and for a while kept on the previous owner as manager, though sacked him when she found he was claiming to be the brains behind the business.

When she died aged 88, extremely rich, she left money to many of her female relatives and friends, stipulating that they and not their husbands should have control of it. Her obituary even appeared in the Gentleman's Magazine, a rare honour for a woman.

It was thought that Eleanor took her secret Coade stone recipe to her grave, but in recent years a few potters have managed to crack the formula. One of the first was the Portobello based potter who helped restore Portobello's Coade Stone Pillars and made the mile markers which denote the underfoot distance along the Portobello promenade (see *Secret Edinburgh* in this series of guides).

FORMER SITE OF THE SÃO CRISTÓVÃO GATEWAY

SYON HOUSE GATEWAY (UNITED KINGOM)

MUSEU DO SAMBA

9

1296 Avenida Visconde de Niterói
Mangueira
• Open Monday to Friday 10am–5pm
• Admission: R$10 (students R$2)
• Bus: 402, 665
• Reservation by phone: (21) 3234-5777
• www.museudosamba.org.br

> *Everything
> you ever wanted
> to know
> about samba*

The Samba Museum is located at the foot of Mangueira district, home to the Estação Primeira de Mangueira (one of the city's most traditional samba schools), in a hangar that was abandoned until 2003, when it was sold to the museum for renovation.

The museum tours are led by researchers who introduce the exhibitions and give information about little-known aspects of samba and its major figures. For those who want to dig deeper, we recommend asking for the Vivência do Samba (Living the Samba) programme: this includes the guided tour, a samba workshop with players and dancers, and the opportunity to try on Carnaval costumes and eat *feijoada* (bean and meat stew) prepared by a Mangueira resident.

The museum has several permanent exhibitions, such as Samba Patrimônio Cultural do Brasil, which presents the history of samba and honours its protagonists. In addition to explanatory texts (in Portuguese) and photographs, it includes costumes donated by the *sambistas*. There are also displays entitled Simplesmente Cartola (Cartola, Quite Simply) on the life of the famous Angenor de Oliveira, known as Cartola, one of the founders of the samba school in 1928, and another on Dona Zica da Mangueira e do Brasil, Cartola's wife. She was a leading female figure in the Mangueira samba school and neighbourhood.

Looking round the exhibitions and chatting with the guide, you'll learn such things as the reason for the Mangueira colours of green and pink – not because Cartola was a supporter of Fluminense Football Club, as many think, but because these are the colours of the Carnaval dance group of his childhood, Arrepiados, from Laranjeiras.

In the same vein, the museum has a lot more information on samba and the samba schools. Apart from the exhibitions, it has a collection of over a hundred testimonies by *sambistas* and researchers. It also runs courses and workshops in addition to the *rodas* (concerts) organised every second Friday of the month in a large graffiti-covered space that mimics the *favela* ambience.

BASÍLICA MENOR DO IMACULADO CORAÇÃO ⑩ DE MARIA

66 Rua Coração de Maria
Méier
• Train: Méier station
• Open Monday to Friday 6.30am–11am and 6.30pm–8pm, Saturday and Sunday 6.30am–8pm
• Every second Saturday of the month, at 2pm, a traditional Latin (Tridentine) Mass – during which the priest always faces the Blessed Sacrament and may turn his back to the congregation – is held at the altar dedicated to the Sacred Heart
• Tel: (21) 2501-3553

The city's only neo-Moorish church

F ive minutes' walk from Méier station in the north of the city, the spectacular Minor Basilica of the Immaculate Heart of Mary is the only neo-Moorish Roman Catholic church in Rio and one of the few in the country. Definitely worth a visit.

Although the church was built between 1909 and 1917 by the monks of the Consecration of the Missionary Sons of the Immaculate Heart of Mary, the tower was not completed until 1924. The design was by Adolfo Morales de Los Rios, the Spanish architect responsible for some of the city's most iconic buildings, such as the early 20th-century National Museum of Fine Arts.

Behind the two doors in carved rosewood, the impressive interior is in typical neo-Moorish style with coloured mosaics, *azulejos* decorating the walls, ans stained glass with a profusion of geometric details, colours and shapes, such the petals of a rose.

The Méier basilica, which can seat 900 people, is highly sought after for weddings because of its great beauty. Listed by the prefecture in 2009, the building features in a series of postcards from the *Olhos de ver* (Eyes to See) collection launched in 2012 by the city prefecture's Instituto Rio Patrimônio da Humanidade.

ONE OF RIO'S FOUR ROMAN CATHOLIC MINOR BASILICAS

The other three are those of the Imaculada Conceição (Immaculate Conception) in Botafogo, Nossa Senhora de Lourdes (Our Lady of Lourdes) in Vila Isabel and Santa Teresinha do Menino Jesus (Saint Thérèse of the Child Jesus) in Tijuca. This special status is granted by the pope to churches that stand out as a place of pilgrimage and are known for their liturgical zeal, historical significance or architectural and artistic beauty. Pope John XXIII granted the title of minor basilica to the Méier church in 1964.

THE STAR HEXAGRAM: A MAGICAL TALISMAN?

The hexagram – also known as the Star of David or the Shield of David – comprises two interlaced equilateral triangles, one pointing upwards and the other downwards. It symbolises the combination of man's spiritual and human nature.

The six points correspond to the six directions in space (north, south, east and west, together with zenith and nadir) and also refer to the complete universal cycle of the six days of creation (the seventh day being when the Creator rested).

Hence, the hexagram became the symbol of the macrocosm (its six angles of 60° totalling 360°) and of the union between mankind and its creator.

Although present in the synagogue of Capernaum (third century AD), the hexagram does not really make its appearance in rabbinical literature until 1148 – in the *Eshkol Hakofer* written by the Karaite* scholar Judah Ben Elijah. In Chapter 242 its mystical and apotropaic (evil-averting) qualities are described, with the actual words then often being engraved on amulets: "And the names of the seven angels were written on the *mazuzah*: The Everlasting will protect you and this symbol called the Shield of David contains, at the end of the *mezuzah*, the written name of all the angels."

In the thirteenth century the hexagram also became an attribute of one of the seven magic names of Metatron, the angel of the divine presence associated with the archangel Michael (head of the heavenly host and the closest to God the Father).

The identification of Judaism with the Star of David began in the Middle Ages. In 1354 King Karel IV of Bohemia granted the Jewish community of Prague the privilege of putting the symbol on their banner. The Jews embroidered a gold star on a red background to form a standard that became known as the Flag of King David (*Maghen David*) and was adopted as the official symbol of Jewish synagogues. By the nineteenth century, the symbol had spread throughout the Jewish community. Jewish mysticism has it that the origin of the hexagram was directly linked with the flowers that adorn the *menorah***: irises with six petals. For those who believe this origin, the hexagram came directly from the hands of the God of Israel, the six-petal iris not only resembling the Star of David in general form but also being associated with the people of Israel in the *Song of Songs*.

As well as offering protection, the hexagram was believed to have magical powers. This reputation originates in the famous *Clavicula Salomonis* (Key of Solomon), a grimoire (textbook of magic) attributed to Solomon himself but, in all likelihood, produced during the Middle Ages. The anonymous texts probably came from one of the numerous Jewish schools of the Kabbalah that then existed in Europe, for the work is clearly inspired by the teachings of the Talmud and the Jewish faith.

The *Clavicula* contains a collection of thirty-six pentacles (themselves symbols rich in magic and esoteric significance) which were intended to enable communication between the physical world and the different levels of the soul.

There are various versions of the text, in numerous translations, and the content varies between them.

However, most of the surviving texts date from the sixteenth and seventeenth centuries – although there is a Greek translation dating from the fifteenth.

In Tibet and India, the Buddhists and Hindus read this universal symbol of the hexagram in terms of the creator and his creation, while the Brahmins hold it to be the symbol of the god Vishnu.

Originally, the two triangles were in green (upright triangle) and red (inverted triangle). Subsequently, these colours became black and white, the former representing the spirit, the latter the material world. For the Hindus, the upright triangle is associated with Shiva, Vishnu and Brahma (corresponding to the Christian God the Father, Son and Holy Ghost).

The Son (Vishnu) can be seen to always occupy the middle position, being the intercessor between things divine and things earthly.

The hexagram also often appears in the windows and pediments of Christian churches, as a symbolic reference to the universal soul. In this case, that soul is represented by Christ – or, sometimes, by the pair of Christ (upright triangle) and the Virgin (inverted triangle); the result of the interlacing of the two is God the Father Almighty. The hexagram is also found in the mediated form of a lamp with six branches or a six-section rose window.

qara'im or bnei mikra: "he who follows the Scriptures". Karaism is a branch of Judaism that defends the sole authority of the Hebrew Scripture as the source of divine revelation, thus repudiating oral tradition.
**Menorah – the multibranched candelabra used in the rituals of Judaism. The arms of the seven-branched menorah, one of the oldest symbols of the Jewish faith, represent the seven archangels before the Throne of God: Michael, Gabriel, Samuel, Raphael, Zadkiel, Anael and Kassiel.

MUSEU DE IMAGENS DO INCONSCIENTE ⓫

521 Rua Ramiro Magalhães
Engenho de Dentro
• Open Monday to Friday 9am–4.30pm
• Tel: (21) 3111-7471

**A must
for those
who love art brut
and research into
the subconscious**

The Museum of Images of the Subconscious was founded in 1952 by psychiatrist Nise da Silveira (1905–1999) to conserve artwork produced in the occupational therapy workshops she had set up (see below).

The life of this exceptional woman, the subject of Roberto Berliner's 2015 film *Nise: O coração da loucura (Nise: The Heart of Madness)*, is difficult to sum up. The only woman among 157 men at the University of Bahia, she was accused of communism during the years of the Vargas dictatorship when she came to work in Rio de Janeiro, imprisoned, then banned from practising for eight years. She rebelled against new psychiatric treatments such as electroshock and lobotomy, refusing to use them, and in 1946 opened a therapeutic occupational service at the Pedro II Psychiatric Centre (now Instituto Municipal Nise da Silveira). Painting and modelling workshops were set up where the patients "occupied" their own workspaces – as can still be seen today. Here the inmates, mostly chronic schizophrenics whom da Silveira called her "clients", were offered a new form of expression and psychiatric treatment. Despite being in open conflict with her colleagues, she received support and recognition from personalities such as eminent Swiss psychiatrist Carl Gustav Jung and leading Brazilian art critic Mário Pedrosa.

Pedrosa was instinctively convinced of the talent of some of da Silveira's "clients". He wrote reference works on what he called "virgin art", a similar concept to French artist Jean Dubuffet's, who coined the term *art brut* to describe the creations of people with no formal artistic background. Pedrosa even wanted to bring the artworks to Rio's Museum of Modern Art but met with strong opposition from da Silveira, who wanted to keep them in "her" museum near the workshops where they were made.

The museum has collected about 350,000 pieces over the sixty years of its existence, some of which have been shown at over 100 exhibitions worldwide. The occupational therapy workshops continue and some of the "clients" exhibit their work alongside internationally recognised names: look out for Emygdio de Barros, Adelina Gomes, Isaac Liberato, Carlos Perthuis and Fernando Diniz, among others.

MUSEU DA VIDA

Fundação Oswaldo Cruz (Fiocruz)
4365 Avenida Brasil
Manguinhos
• Open Tuesday to Friday 9am–4.30pm, reservation by phone (2590-6747 – not required Saturday 10am–4pm), tours in Portuguese only
• Admission free
• Tel: (21) 2598-4242
• http://portal.fiocruz.br/pt-br/content/museu-da-vida
• Bus: several lines (e.g. 483, 292, 320, 300) serve Fiocruz, but taxi recommended

Science is life

L ocated on the Oswaldo Cruz Foundation (Fiocruz) campus, with 35,000 m^2 of green space, historic buildings and scientific research installations, the Museum of Life runs many unusual activities around the theme of the human body.

The museum, which opened on 25 May 1999, also has a small butterfly house colonised by four species from the Americas. The guided tours present the life of butterflies, providing minute details of their life cycle and eating habits, and the secrets behind their varied colours and survival strategies. Sometimes butterflies settle on the visitors.

A variety of games and experiments on microscopic or macroscopic lives and the perception of light and sound are also offered in the Biodiscovery Hall. You can examine a giant model of the human eye and, under the direction of the guides, learn how images are formed.

Microscopes are provided for children and adults to observe the "workshop of the micro-world" of insects and human tissues. It's also very interesting to try making models of cells with the materials supplied, which you're sometimes allowed to take home.

Through experiments and interactive games, visitors aged 9 and above can

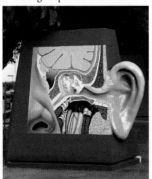

learn about the role of physics in the explanation of certain phenomena: how can vision be deceptive, making us perceive a movement instead of a static image?

How is it possible to see colours where there was previously only black and white?

GUIDED TOUR OF PAVILHÃO MOURISCO

Fundação Oswaldo Cruz (Oswaldo Cruz Foundation – Fiocruz)
4365 Avenida Brasil
Manguinhos
• Tel: (21) 2598-4242 • portal.fiocruz.br
• Open Tuesday to Friday 9am–4.30pm, reservation by phone (2590-6747 – not required Saturday 10am–4pm), tours in Portuguese only
• Admission free
• Bus: several lines (e.g. 483, 292, 320, 300) serve Fiocruz, but taxi recommended

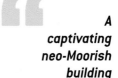

A captivating neo-Moorish building

On the way from Galeao International Airport to the Zona Sul, five to ten minutes from the airport, you'll notice an imposing building on the horizon to the right: the beautiful Moorish Pavilion is the headquarters of the Oswaldo Cruz Foundation. Built between 1905 and 1918, it is listed as national heritage. Contrary to what you might think, it is open to the public.

The building was designed by Dr Oswaldo Cruz (1872–1917), a noted physician and epidemiologist, and is one of Brazil's very few neo-Moorish monuments.

It uses a harmonious blend of materials from many countries: the bricks, tiles and stuccowork are French, the marble originally from Italy, the *azulejos*

Portuguese, the lighting fixtures German, the metalwork English, including the beautiful staircase, the windows Belgian and the woodwork Brazilian. The elevator, installed in 1909, is the oldest still operating in the city.

The bathrooms on all floors are stacked in a tower, accessible from the building but not part of the main construction, to avoid any cross-contamination.

The pavilion contains mysteries that feed the imagination of those who work there or visit. There is talk of footsteps or strange noises at night when everyone is gone; doors slamming even when they're closed; and a book that someone is looking for spontaneously appearing right in front of them. Not to mention the story of the night guard on his rounds, who went to the third-floor library at dawn and found a man dressed in white sitting there. The terrified guard collapsed before making a run for it.

The surrounding area was a swamp (now filled in), which is why the area is called Manguinhos, meaning "little swamp".

THE HIDDEN FLOOR

Seen from the outside, the building appears to have four floors. In fact there are five – there's another before the top floor, windowless (designed as a darkroom), which is why you would never guess it was there. Photographer J. Pinto worked there from 1903 to 1946 to record the production of serums and vaccines, in addition to his research and teaching activities.

THE SPLENDID READING ROOM OF THE RARE BOOKS COLLECTION

On the third floor of the building, the rare books section of the library is a magnificent space, fully preserved, with dark-brown Brazilian walnut (*imbuia*) wood furniture, cast iron and bronze light fittings, with German-made accessories in lilac opal. The wooden flooring consists of geometric shapes in various shades, the walls and ceiling feature pretty ornaments in white plaster. The collection includes works from the 17th century, such as the first treatise on the natural history of Brazil by Willem Piso and Georg Marggraf, *Naturalis historia brasiliae*, dating from 1648. The reading room is open to visitors, but only researchers are allowed to consult the books.

TREM DO SAMBA

Every year, first Saturday in December: first train for guests leaves at
6.04pm, followed by four others at twenty-minute intervals
Central do Brasil station to Oswaldo Cruz
• www.tremdosamba.com.br
• Free

Contagious joy

The fantastic Samba Train, inaugurated in 1996, is a project of singer and composer Marquinhos from the Oswaldo Cruz neighbourhood: he wanted to commemorate National Samba Day and restore the former glory of this traditional musical genre. These trains run once a year in the early evening of the first Saturday in December, to mark National Samba Day, which is celebrated on the 2nd of the same month.

The day of festivities begins in an atmosphere of contagious joy at Central Station, with a great free show around midday. On the way to Oswaldo Cruz (thirty minutes by train), a different samba band plays in each carriage.

On arrival, the musicians perform for free on stage or during more informal *rodas de samba* shows, in bars or on the street corners of this district considered the mecca of traditional Carioca samba.

A TRAIN INSPIRED BY THE *FÊTE DE LA MUSIQUE* IN PARIS

Oswaldo Cruz concerts started in the second year of the Samba Train, when Marquinhos learned of the music festival held every 21 June in Paris, and felt that there was nothing better than samba musicians to greet the arrival of the train.

WHY 6.04PM?

The first Samba Train for invited guests, with Marquinhos and representatives of the old guard of Rio's traditional samba schools, always starts at 6.04pm in memory of the fact that, in the 1930s, it was the train that Paulo da Portela caught every day on his way home. During the trip, Paulo and his friends sang and played, taking advantage of the lack of police repression at a time when the samba was banned. After the 6.04 train, four others leave Central Station, one every twenty minutes.

Paulo da Portela, real name Paulo Benjamin de Oliveira (1901–1949), singer and composer, was a founder of the Portela samba school – both him and the school were named after the nearby Portela road. Paulo, a major figure of Brazilian culture, fought hard to change the preconceptions surrounding the samba players, depicting them as thugs and vagabonds rather than respected artists. For example, he insisted that the local people should be dressed in the samba school colours on parade day.

MONTE ESCADA DE JACÓ

512 Avenida Mons Felix
Irajá
- Metro: Irajá
- Open 24/7
- Mass Mondays at 9am

A place of powerful spiritual energy?

One of the most astonishing places in Rio lies at the heart of the Zona Norte, a few minutes' walk from Irajá metro – the Mount of Jacob's Ladder, a reference to the episode in the Old Testament.

Until 2010, the hillside was the haunt of prostitutes and the place (known as the "microwave" ...) where traffickers from the surrounding *favelas* came to "liquidate" anybody who'd got in their way.

All this changed on 15 May 2010, when God appeared in a dream to Father Marcelo Flores, of the Igreja Evangélica Assembléia de Deus (Evangelical Church of the Assembly of God), commanding him to transform the site into a place of spirituality. Following this dream, Father Marcelo opened his Bible at the passage describing Jacob's ladder (see below), and so he named the hill.

With the help of friends, Father Marcelo, who lives nearby, cleaned up the site (which belongs to the army) and began to paint the stones white. Verses from the Bible were added to some of them.

From then on, this became one of Rio's most fervent prayer and meditation venues. Depending on the time of day (busiest Monday morning and Friday evening, as well as Saturday evening and Sunday afternoon), you'll meet people praying alone or in groups, kneeling facing the city, quietly reading the Bible, or others, more active, who come along to chat with other believers.

Although the site is mainly frequented by Evangelists, other denominations are also welcome.

THE BIBLICAL STORY OF JACOB'S LADDER

Jacob's dream is an episode of the Book of Genesis (28: 10–19) that begins as follows: "Jacob left Beersheba, and set out for Harran. When he reached a certain place, he stopped for the night because the sun had set. Taking one of the stones there, he put it under his head and lay down to sleep. He had a dream in which he saw a stairway resting on the earth, with its top reaching to heaven, and the angels of God were ascending and descending on it."

GALPÃO BELA MARÉ

(16)

169 Rua Bittencourt Sampaio, Maré
Between footbridges 9 and 10 of Avenida Brasil
• Open Tuesday to Friday 10am–5pm, Saturday 11am–5pm
• Admission free
• Tel: (21) 3105-4599 / 3105-1148 • www.travessias.org.br

**Contemporary
art in Maré favela**

Many Carioca *favelas* support cultural projects that showcase the knowledge and creativity of their residents. Their quality and inventiveness are such that they are sometimes included in cultural itineraries around the city and are well worth a visit. This applies to Maré, near the international airport, where several former large warehouses are now given over to the arts. One of them is home to projects designed by the great choreographer, Lia Rodrigues; another houses the Travessias (Crossings) project, dedicated to the visual arts.

Travessias was set up by the historian, editor and producer Luiza Mello and Jorge Barbosa, one of the directors of Observatório de Favelas (www.observatoriodefavelas.org.br). This ambitious civil society research organisation, with headquarters in Maré since 2001, works on urban policy, education, culture and human rights. Interventions in popular places are fundamental to the organisation. The Travessias project, launched in 2011, invited art critics and/or renowned visual artists to design exhibitions with and about the community of Maré.

Artist residencies allow for "anthropological" participatory work between creators and the local people, who are always associated with the educational

activities and discussions that form part of a project.

The beautiful Galpão (warehouse) Bela Maré provides public access to a library of art books. Architect Pedro Evora has been working for several years on a large model of Maré that you can see on the first floor. For art lovers, a few of the artists who've been involved since the beginning of this fine adventure are worth a mention: Ernesto Neto, Vik Muniz, Daniel Senise, Regina Silveira, Carlos Vergara ...

MUSEU DA MARÉ

26 Avenida Guilherme Maxwell, Maré
• Tel: (21) 3868-6748 • museudamare.org.br
• Open Tuesday to Saturday 9am–6pm, visits on reservation, some guided tours
• Suggested contribution: R$6
• Bus: 378, 393, 397 (from Zone Sul or Centro, take the bus at Central Station as far as walkway 7 on Avenida Brasil, then walk around 700 m to the museum)

The first favela museum

The Maré Museum is installed in a warehouse formerly used for marine repairs. Although it's not very large – around 600 m² – it means a great deal to the population of the sixteen communities that make up the Maré *favela* complex. Opened in May 2006, the museum is the follow-up to a community project launched in 1989 to record local residents' images and experiences.

A panel at the entrance defines the aims of the museum: "It's not a place for preserving objects or worshipping the past. It's a place of life … where the past, present and future live in harmony." This panel is painted in a clay-like colour to emphasise that the first inhabitants of the *favela*, mainly poor migrants from rural areas in the Northeast, came to Rio de Janeiro in search of a better life but were only able to settle in the run-down or flood-prone areas around Guanabara bay.

Next, in a large space, is a replica of a *palafita* (wooden hut on stilts), essential for living in the flooded Maré. The objects and furniture of this lakeside building were donated by local people from the things they used at home. Clothes are hanging up as if they were drying in the sun, and through the hut windows archive footage reveals the *favela* landscape as it was before the urbanisation scheme of the 1980s, when the *palafitas* were eradicated.

The museum is organised into twelve sections (water, housing, migration, resistance, work, festivals, markets, faith, daily life, children, fear and the future) represented by an installation that includes, for example, tools, photos, toys and everyday items donated or made by community members. The installations tell the story of the *favela* and its people, with their struggles and aspirations.

In addition to the permanent exhibition, the museum houses archives for research and the dissemination of local history, a library and an artisanal products and sales project. The guides are young people from Maré, trained in association with local universities.

IGREJA DO BOM JESUS DA COLUNA

Cidade Universitária
Ilha do Fundão
• Tel: (21) 2519-5352
• Access: private car or taxi
• Sunday Mass 10am
• Admission free

A forgotten colonial gem

The church of Good Jesus of the Column, built in 1705 according to the inscription on the cloister door, is a real colonial gem with national heritage status. Built as part of a Franciscan convent, the church is out in the countryside on a military range (to reach it, you have to pass through a control point – ID needed), with beautiful views over Guanabara bay.

Like one or two of Rio's other splendid ecclesiastical buildings – the Benedictine Abbey of Our Lady of Montserrat, more commonly known as the Mosteiro de São Bento; and Lapa dos Mercadores, the Traders' Church of Our Lady of Lapa – the church has a narthex (enclosed porch at the entrance). Between the bell tower and the sacristy, on the right, the cloister corridor has two floors topped by arches (all that's left of the convent).

The interior of the church is notable for the simplicity of its smooth walls, but the main and side altars are late Rococo in style. Facing the chapel is the richly decorated stele of Antônio Teles de Menezes and his descendants, the former owners of the land ceded to the Franciscans (the same family that built the Arco de Teles on the site of the old pillory in Praça XV).

In the crypt, in front of the ossuary of the Teles de Menezes family, is a secret passage that allowed the monks to escape to a part of the island protected by rocky outcrops in case of an attack from the sea – a sort of emergency exit leading to a cove. Enemy ships could easily be spotted from the church, which enjoyed a wide view of Guanabara bay.

It was in this church that the feast day of St Francis of Assisi was celebrated, which is why João VI was a frequent visitor to the island when he lived in Brazil. After independence, the government took over the island and the convent dependencies were used as a lazaretto, a hostel for immigrants and a barracks. Then in 1868 an asylum, now abandoned, was built closer to the sea (Asilo dos Inválidos da Pátria) for the wounded servicemen of the Paraguayan War. The church has been luckier and continues to attract worshippers, mostly soldiers.

The church of Bom Jesus da Coluna was built in the 18th century on what was then Ilha do Bom Jesus, part of a small archipelago of eight islands. In the early 1950s the embankment that links all the islands was completed and extended to Fundão, about 3 million m², to accommodate the Federal University of Rio de Janeiro (UFRJ). The site now houses major research and technology centres.

MARGAY CAT STATUE

⑲

End of Guanabara beach
Ilha do Governador
• Bus: 634

The maracajá of Paranapuã

On Governor's Island off Guanabara beach, a statue of the *maracajá*, the Indian term for the wild cats that existed in the 16th century, stands on Pedra da Onca (Jaguar rock), which owes its name to the statue because of the marked similarity between the *maracajá* (margay or tiger cat) and the jaguar. The rock was also known as Pedra dos Amores (Lovers' rock).

The statue is said to have been inspired by a legend, which started with a young woman from the island's Temiminó tribe who had a pet *maracajá*. Every afternoon she took it to the beach and dived from the rock, while the wild cat watched her. One day, the legend goes, she was drowned and the *maracajá* waited for her on the rock until it died. Like any legend there may be no truth in it, but it has inspired the local people. In the 1920s, they decided to build a monument to immortalise this story, symbol of friendship, loyalty and hope. A local artist, Guttman Bicho, designed the concrete cat that was later installed on the largest of the rounded rocks at the end of Guanabara beach. The statue crumbled over time, so on 20 January 1965, the feast day of St Sebastian, patron of the city (see p. 127), it was replaced by another which still stands there today.

Despite the pollution in the bay, the site of the statue is exquisite: on one side, a small wooded area and, on the other, a little beach frequented by swimmers and fishers. The view is superb: as well as the panorama over the bay, you can see in the distance the peak of Dedo de Deus (Finger of God), the mountainous area of Teresópolis.

ILHA DO GATO
While the indigenous people called the place Ilha de Paranapuã (meaning "round sea"), the Portuguese, until the late 1560s, knew it as Ilha do Gato (Cat Island), perhaps in reference to the large numbers of *maracajá* living there. The name Ilha do Governador only appeared in 1567 after Mem de Sá, governor-general of the Portuguese colony, handed over much of the island to his great-grandson Salvador Correia de Sá (appointed governor of the captaincy of Rio de Janeiro in 1568).

WHERE DOES GALEÃO AIRPORT'S NAME COME FROM?
Another governor, Salvador Correa de Sá e Benevides, installed a shipyard on the island that in 1663 built the *Galeão Padre Eterno*, considered at the time to be the largest ship in the world. The site remained known as Ponta do Galeão (galleon), which subsequently gave its name to the international airport.

CEMITÉRIO DOS PÁSSAROS

Rua Manoel de Macedo
Ilha de Paquetá
Boats to Paquetá throughout the day from Praça XV, downtown Rio
• Timetable and fares at www.grupoccr.com.br/barcas/linhas-horarios-tarifas

> **The world's only known bird cemetery**

In the quiet Rua Manoel de Macedo, next to Paquetá cemetery, is a burial ground for birds, the only one in the world. The handful of graves are all identical: the tradition is that owners of dead birds check the available space among the graves (over time, the bodies decompose into the earth), and there they lay to rest the creature that kept them company during its lifetime.

Modern legislation on the protection of wild life means that fewer and fewer people keep wild animals in captivity, which is why there is a reduction in the number of "funerals". But since its establishment by local artist Pedro Bruno (1888–1949), in addition to being a cemetery, this wooded and serene area is also an ode to the love of nature, as residents will confirm.

As well as the tombs and two monuments – "The shot bird" and "Landing of the tired bird" – one wall has short poems by well-known and unknown writers. The cemetery also has seats and little tables, which are very popular in this neighbourhood meeting place.

BRAZIL'S FIRST NUDIST CLUB

Paquetá is the second largest island in Guanabara bay. It has also given its name to an archipelago of eighteen islands and *matações* (rounded rocks that look like small islands). In the 1950s, the controversial Brazilian artist Luz del Fuego (1917–1967) set up the country's first nudist club on the island of Sol.

HOW CAN YOU BE SURE OF YOUR PARTNER'S LOVE?

Paquetá and its many nicknames, such as the Island of Love or the Pearl of Guanabara, have inspired several romantic traditions. To be sure of your partner's love, go to the Pedra dos Namorados (Lovers' Rock), at the tip of Praia José Bonifácio, and throw three small stones, from behind you, on top of the rock, while thinking about your great love. If at least one of them stays up on the rock, then your passion is mutual. And if you want to find love, just sip the water of São Roque well and someone on the island will succumb to your charms.

Since 1967, Paquetá has had ten trees listed by municipal decree. In addition to a baobab, there are almond, mango, tamarind and jackfruit trees.

TUNNELS AND CAVES OF PARQUE DARKE DE **㉑** MATTOS

Ilha de Paquetá, at the end of Praia José
Bonifácio
• Open daily 8am—5pm
• Free
• Boats to Paquetá throughout the day from Praça XV, downtown Rio
Timetable and fares at www.grupoccr.com.br/barcas/linhas-horarios-
tarifas

Signs
of kaolin mining

t the end of José Bonifácio beach, on the beautiful island of Paquetá, Darke de Mattos park offers visitors stunning views of the bay, ancient trees and unusual tunnels and caves which are the remains of kaolin mines (a type of white clay used in making porcelain). Although this is a 20th-century park with lawns and a children's playground, it's also a fine example of the Romantic landscaped garden that was much in vogue in the 19th century.

Paths lead to the top of the small Morro da Cruz (Hill of the Cross) and its belvedere. Most of the caves resulting from the clay excavations can be found along these paths. They are all shapes and sizes: while some are large enough to enter, they're dark inside, so it's not a good idea to venture in alone and without a light.

At the far end of the park, a boardwalk offers a stunning view of the bay, with Ilha do Governador (Governor's Island) in the distance. Nearby, at a slightly higher level, is perhaps the most surprising feature of the gardens: a short tunnel dug in the hillside which opens onto a small and pretty beach – for children, it's like discovering an uninhabited island. Horses are often to be seen on the beach, which is near the stables of the horses that pull the traditional Paquetá carts.

Although there was once a thriving farm in the region, it closed in 1747. Later, the Jesuits made porcelain with the clay from the hill and, at the end of the 19th century, a weaving mill was in operation here.

The land was purchased in the early 20th century by the entrepreneur Darke de Mattos, who had a large house built with a pool and a hangar for the seaplanes he piloted. All this has disappeared. His daughter donated the property to the prefecture, which converted it into a park.

Prince Regent Dom João often went to Paquetá. His first visit, in late 1808, came about quite by chance when his ship ran aground during a wild storm on one of the island's beaches. Despite turning up so unexpectedly, he enjoyed a warm welcome. Dom João returned there again and again and, during one of his stays, he was presented with a set of china made from the local clay.

INDEX ALPHABÉTIQUE

INDEX ALPHABÉTIQUE